HISTORY AND GEOGRAPHY

Creation to Modern Israel

A TIMELINE STUDY

Leona England Karni

Copyright © 2016 by Leona England Karni. All rights reserved.

Creation to Modern Israel: A Timeline Study by Leona England Karni

Create Space (a division of Amazon.com) functions only as book publisher. As such, the ultimate design, content, editorial accuracy, and views expressed or implied in this work are those of the author.

No part of this publication may be reproduced, stored in a retrieval system or transmitted in any way by any means—electronic, mechanical, photocopy, recording or otherwise—without the prior permission of the copyright holder, except as provided by USA copyright law.

Unless otherwise noted, all Scriptures are taken from the King James Version of the Holy Bible.

Cover design by Sylvia D. Coleman
Front-cover photograph credits with permission to use:
    Sylvia D. Coleman: "Glory in the Clouds"
    Wayne McLean, "Jerusalem from the Mt. of Olives" (2005), (photograph adapted); Mr. McLean does not necessarily endorse this Timeline Study or its use.

Printed in the United States of America

ISBN-10: 1532849672
ISBN-13: 978-1532849671

CONTENTS

Acknowledgements xiii
Introduction xv
Note to Instructor xvii

CHAPTER ONE 1
  INTRODUCTION 1
    Fertile Crescent 3
    Hand Drawn Map of Israel 5
    Routes and Passes 6
      International Coastal Highway/Via Maris 6
      Via Maris Coastal Highway 6
      King's Highway 6
      Central Ridge Route 7
      Beth Horon Ridge Route (BHRR) 7
      Kishon Pass 7
      Aruna Mountain Pass 7
    Valleys 8
      Aijalon Valley (AV) 8
      Elah Valley 8
      Sorek Valley 8
      Guverian Valley 8
    Climate and Agriculture 9
    Rains 9
    Mountains 9
    Dews 10
    Rainfall 10
    Winds 11
    Crops 11
    References 13

CHAPTER TWO 15
  CREATION TO THE FALL 15
    Challenges of Ancient History 16
    Dating 16
      Carbon Dating-The Premise 17
      Carbon Dating-The Controversy 17
    Bias of Researchers 17

- New Discoveries 18
- Oopart 18
- Creation 19
- Gap Theory 20
- Declaration of War 21
- Lucifer 21
- Formal Declaration of War 23
- Mitochondrial Eve 25
- The Garden 25
- Genesis 5 26
- References 27

CHAPTER THREE 29
- FLOOD TO SHECHEM 29
- Sons of God and the Daughters of Man 29
- The Flood: Second Environmental Change 32
  - Genesis 6-10 32
- Table of Nations 33
  - Genesis 10 33
- Division of Languages 34
- Mesopotamia and the UR of Chaldees 35
  - Sumer-Akkad 35
  - Concept of King Develops 36
  - Akkadians (2300BC) 38
  - Abram 38
  - Dating Abram's Arrival 39
- Amorites – 1900—2000 BC) 40
  - Origins 40
  - Effects on Mesopotamia 41
  - Alternative View 41
  - Amorite Father 41
  - Elamites Conquer 42
- Shechem 42
  - Jacob 43
  - Moses 44
  - Joshua 44
  - Joseph 44
  - Abimelech 44
  - Rehoboam-Jeroboam 44
- Samaria 45
  - Woman at the Well 45
- REFEERENCES 46

CHAPTER FOUR 47
PATRIARCHAL AGE: WILDERNESS WANDERINGS 47
Patriarchal Age 47
- Genesis 14 47
Tribes in the Land 48
- Kenites 49
- Midianites 50
- Rechabites 51
Historical Accounts 1160 and 1828 BC 51
- Wilderness Wanderings 52
- Kadesh-barnea 53
- Mt. Hor 54
- Arad 54
- Hormah 55
- Edom 55
- Obadiah 55
- Second Temple Period 56
REFERENCES 57

CHAPTER FIVE 59
CONQUEST TO JUDGES 59
Entering the Land and the Conquest 59
- Crossing the Jordan 60
- Gilgal 60
- Ai 62
- Gibeonites (Joshua 9) 62
- Biblical Amorites 64
- Joshua Ten 64
- Time of the Judges 66
- Local Enemies 67
- Moabites 67
- Ruth 68
REFERENCES 69

CHAPTER SIX 70
PRIESTS AND LEVITES 70
SAMUEL-SOLOMON 70
Priests 70
- Decoding the Priesthood 70
Levites 71
Samuel 73
Prophets 73

Shiloh 74
Philistines Capture the Ark 75
Men at Beth-Shemesh 75
Saul 1052—1010 BC 76
David - 1010—970 BC 76
Solomon 970—930 BC 77
Syria and Egypt 78
REFERENCES 78

CHAPTER SEVEN 81
DIVIDED KINGDOM-CAPTIVITY 81
Assyria-Babylon-Egypt 82
Ashur-dan II: 935—912 BC 82
Mt. Arbel 82
Divided Kingdom: 909—886 BC 83
Armenia 83
Israel-Assyria 84
Syro Ephraim War - 740 BC 87
Isaiah Prophesies 87
During the Syro-Ephraimite War 87
Israel - Northern Kingdom 88
Ten Northern Tribes 89
Samaritans 89
Sennacherib (704—681 BC) 90
Judah 90
Josiah – 673 BC 92
Jehoiakim 93
Zedekiah 94
Gedaliah ben Ahikam 94
Three Deportations 94
REFERENCES 95

CHAPTER EIGHT 97
BABYLONIAN CAPTIVITY: THE RETURN 97
Judaism Prior to Captivity 98
Development of Judaism in Captivity 100
Prophets in Exile 102
Babylonian Empire 102
Medo-Persia Empire 103
The Return: Zerubbabel - Cyrus 538—520 BC 103
Esther - Ahasuerus (Xerxes I) 486—465 BC 103
Ezra 104

viii

Xerxes (Ahasuerus) 486—465 BC, Esther 104
Artaxerxes II 464—425 BC - Nehemiah 2 105
Summary *106*
REFERENCES *107*

CHAPTER NINE 109
SECOND TEMPLE PERIOD 109
Judaism Transformed *109*
Persia *111*
Macedon-Greece *111*
Alexander III - Alexander the Great 356—323 BC *112*
Alexander the Great at Jerusalem *113*
Israel *114*
Alexandria *114*
Conclusion *115*
REFERENCES *116*

CHAPTER TEN 117
SELEUCIDS, PTOLEMIES AND MACCABEES 117
Rome on the Rise *118*
Hellenized Jews *118*
Mattathias and Sons *120*
REFERENCES *124*

CHAPTER ELEVEN 125
HASMONEAN AND HERODIAN DYNASTIES: 164—63 BC 125
Political Parties *126*
Pharisees Taught 127
Services: Community Houses-Synagogues 127
Sadducees 128
Herodian Dynasty *129*
Antigonus and the Parthians 130
Herod the Great - Family Tree 132
REFERENCES *133*

CHAPTER TWELVE 135
THE TRIUMPHAL ENTRY 135
Palm Sunday *135*
REFERENCES *138*

CHAPTER THIRTEEN 139
DAILY SERVICE IN THE TEMPLE 139
Preparation for Passover *139*

- DURING THE TIME OF JESUS: Ceremonial Cleansing 142
- Room for the Last Supper 143
- Sacrifice at the Temple 144
- REFERENCES 146

CHAPTER FOURTEEN 147
THE PASSOVER 147
- Needed for a Traditional Passover Seder 150
- At the Time of Jesus 151
- *The Order of the Passover Service* *151*
  - Jesus Institutes Communion 161
  - Elijah the Prophet 163
  - REFERENCES 165

CHAPTER FIFTEEN 167
PILATE 167
- *First Citizens of Rome* *167*
- *Pontius Pilate* *167*
- *The Standards* *171*
- *The Aqueduct* *172*
- *The Aspiedeion* *173*
- *Inquisitorial System* *173*
- *Pilate in Jerusalem* *174*
- *The Trial and Crucifixion* *174*
- REFERENCES 177

CHAPTER SIXTEEN 179
OLD TESTAMENT FEASTS 179
DAY OF REST 179
- *Traditional Observances for Shabbath* *181*
  - Lighting the Candles 181
  - Blessing 181
  - Synagogue 182
  - Washing of the Hands 182
  - Kiddush 182
  - Blessing over the Challah 182
  - Salt Covenant 183
  - Meal 183
  - Blessing after the Meal 183
  - Traditional Prayers 184
  - The Going Out of the Sabbath 184
- *Commandments Concerning the Sabbath* *184*
- *New Moon* *185*

- Time Measured 185
- Names of the Months 186
- Year 187
- New Moon 187
- Rabbinical Writings and Thoughts 188
- *Pilgrim Feasts* *188*
  - First Fruits 189
  - Feast of Harvest-Shavuot - Counting the Omer 189
  - Feast of the Trumpets - Rosh ha Shanna 190
  - Day of Atonement - Yom Kippur 191
  - Kol Nidre 191
  - Feast of Tabernacles - Succoth 192
- *REFERENCES* *194*

CHAPTER SEVENTEEN 195
JUDAISM & THE EARLY CHURCH 195
Nazarenes *195*
Early Disciples *195*
Rome and the Jews *197*
- Political Rivalry among the Jews 197
- Final Cause 198
- Josephus 199
- Triumphal Procession 200
Early Church *200*
- Church Unity 202
- Church Councils - Acts 15 203
- Discussion and Issues of the Early Church 203
- Further Discussions of the Early Church Fathers 204
- Armenian Apostolic Church 205
- Assyrian Orthodox Church 205
- Persecuted Church - Diocletian 206
Constantine *206*
Byzantine Empire *209*
- 324—610 AD 209
- 610—1081 AD 209
- 1081—1453 AD 210
- *REFERENCES* *212*

CHAPTER EIGHTEEN 213
MODERN ISRAEL 213
Zionism *213*
- Factors in the Development of Zionism 214

    Beliefs of Zionism 214
    World War I - 1914—1918..*216*
    1919 Arab Literary Club and Arab Club............................*217*
    US Limits Immigration (rations) - 1924............................*218*
    World War II *220*
        War of Independence..221
        Population Transfer 222
        REFERENCES..*223*

CHAPTER NINETEEN... **225**
  PALESTINIANS AND THE ARAB-ISRAELI CONFLICT 225
    Palestine-Southern Syria *225*
        The Disaster (War of Independence).........................226
        Occupied West Bank...226
        Military Occupation 227
        What is a Palestinian? 227
        Who Are the Palestinians? 228
        Christian Palestinians 229
        Christian Palestinian Organizations in Israel...............229
    Arab-Israeli Conflict *230*
        Pray for the Peace of Jerusalem 232
        REFERENCES..*233*

Acknowledgements

My very special thanks to Jeanine Michaels and Sylvia Coleman without whom the years of research, compilation of the historical record, teaching, and writing that were needed to complete this Timeline Study in its present form would not have been realized—and to all of you (including teachers and students) who have encouraged me to create this study book.

Introduction

Over the years of teaching on the ancient history of the Holy Land, the questions and interests of my students have directed the development of the course content. For example, most of my students have not been familiar with ancient Mesopotamia (which appears early on the timeline), while at the other end of the timeline is modern Israel and the Arab-Israeli conflict—which has elicited many questions. Thus, the Timeline has evolved to cover *history* and *geography* from Creation to Modern Israel. Obviously, this is not an exhaustive study but rather a guided tour which focuses on points of **historical significance** and suggests areas of further study that may interest the student.

For the serious Bible student, it would be beneficial to revert to the ancient habit of using pen and paper to make your own Timeline. An example of how to do this can be found in the early chapters of this book. This effort, although time consuming, will help in the assimilation of the vast amount of information this course covers and will serve as a quick reference for the context of specific historical events.

All students will benefit from the understanding of historical events that are sometimes seemingly insignificant but have had an impact on ancient Israel, the Early Church and are relevant today. This textbook will help you to "connect the dots" so to speak and give you a greater understanding of the history recorded in the Bible.

Leona England Karni
2016

Note to Instructor

This course was developed to be taught in Bible Colleges over the course of a semester. Taught in a variety of forums, the curriculum may be presented as one to two-week block classes, weekend seminars in a church setting and so on. It is entirely possible to take any part of this course and emphasize only a certain time period. For example, the time between the testaments is a time period in history that is rich with events and developments in Judaism which enhance our understanding of the times of Christ. Another example could be the development of Judaism and Old Testament Feasts and Festivals. If the forum is a block class or a weekend seminar, it will be necessary to choose one time-period upon which to focus.

If teaching in a Bible College, a timeline is developed beginning with Creation and continuing on to Modern Israel. The emphasis on a particular time period depends on the background of the students. For example, students who have a limited background in differing opinions on Creation would benefit from a discussion on New Earth, Six Day Creation, and Old Earth and the Gap Theory. If, however, the students have covered this in a previous class, it is sufficient to place Creation/Genesis 1:1 on the Timeline and move on.

The Timeline should serve as a reference in future studies for the student. Throughout the course, relevant secular events will be incorporated into the Timeline (i.e. secular dates placed above, and the Biblical events and references placed below the line). This will serve as a quick reference in future studies. Therefore, the completed Timeline is a significant portion of the student's grade. If the class spans over an entire semester, a notebook is required that includes a Timeline with references to mark events.

The development of the Notebook is guided by questions that require essay answers. Sample questions might be, "Discuss the differences between the New Earth and Old Earth theories of Creation"; or "Describe the strategic location of Jericho." A three ring binder with clear plastic page covers is suggested for the notebook. Each chapter of this text book will include suggestions for notebook questions.

Classroom Discussion Questions are included in each chapter. These are questions on which scholars are divided because there is no absolute answer found in scripture. For example, "Who were the 'sons of God' referred to in Genesis 6:2?" Participation in these discussions is required and is factored into the grade. The question may be written on the white board or overhead projector at the beginning of class. The students are not given the questions ahead of time, and their opinions should be supported logically. The benefit of this exercise is to encourage or stimulate the students to think about and communicate what they think.

CHAPTER ONE

INTRODUCTION

DISCUSSION QUESTION: Why do we study the Bible?

Isn't it enough to accept Jesus as your personal Savior, repent, be baptized and attend church on Sunday? Why should we have personal Bible Study—why attend a Bible College? I can only answer these questions from my own personal experience. I felt compelled to study the Bible. The Holy Spirit drew me to study, and through the study of God's Word, I grew to know Him, and to know His character. For me personally, I study the Bible to understand the character of God, because when I know and understand His character, I can know His thoughts on matters that pertain to my daily life. And, because I know His character, I can trust Him.

There are various methods and approaches one can use to study the Bible. The Bible is an historical record of antiquity from a Judaic Christian experience. So, to study it as history is reasonable, but it is not just an historical account; it is history with a *purpose*. This history reveals God as Creator and places man in space and time. This history instructs man in what God requires of him. This history guides us in our relationship with Him and instructs us in how we should live. In the study of the Bible from an historical perspective, one takes what is within the pages literally.

But, beyond the literal surface there is a *literary style* to consider. A writing style is the manner in which an author chooses to convey thought—which reveals both the writer's personality and shows how he perceives the reader. Therefore, for a serious study of the Bible, one must become familiar with its literary style. For example, the use of symbolism is threaded throughout the Bible. A symbol is a person, place or thing that represents something else: such as the number four, forty, 400 and so on. These are symbolic of judgment. For example, the children of Israel wandered in the wilderness for forty years because of their unbelief.

Additionally, *typology*, which is a special kind of prophetic symbolism, is found in the Old Testament and is used to foreshadow something or someone in the New Testament. Typology is woven throughout the pages of the Old Testament. One such example is Isaac as a "type" of Christ. He was offered as a sacrifice by his father, and he met his bride in the field (which is symbolic of the world). We are the bride of Christ, dwelling in the world (field).

Another helpful tool to understand is the *literary style of the Bible* in presenting historical accounts. A general context or background is first presented, and then, the focus shifts to what is important in regard to man. For example, in the historical account of creation found in **Genesis 1:26**, we read, "*And God said, Let us make man in our image...*" And then in **Genesis 2:7**, we read, "*And the Lord formed man...*" What is given in chapter one is the overall picture of creation, including the creation of man. In chapter two, the focus is on what is important—man. This is true also in the listing of genealogies. The line which is significant is the line through which Jesus is born. Therefore, the least significant is presented summarily first, then the focus is on the Messianic Line.

We can also study the Bible from a *geographical perspective*: Creator God created the land of Israel, and selected it for His chosen people. GEOGRAPHY (which is the study of the earth's surface—in this case the land of Israel) also reflects the character of God. Therefore, by gaining an understanding of the geographical aspects of the land of the Bible, one can also gain a further understanding of the *Creator*. For instance, God selected the geographical location of Israel for His chosen people. What does His choice tell us about His character? One obvious aspect of His character is His desire to be involved in the daily lives of His people as demonstrated by their need to be in fellowship with Him for protection and for rains in their due season.

The Bible, although written over hundreds of years and by numerous authors, is consistent on all of these levels mentioned. This testifies to the reality that the Bible was inspired by God and reflects the character of God.

Fertile Crescent

In this class our primary focus will be on the history and geography of the area of the lands of the Bible, known as Mesopotamia and the Fertile Crescent. History reflects the character and the nature of people. Geography represents the stage on which the pageant of history is presented.

> "In the place where water gushes from the ground, there also a man drives his tent stake - and so lays the foundation of a city. Where the easiest ground to travel lies, there a wayfarer walks - and so a highway begins. The rains run through immovable ravines, and beside that river people cultivate their fields and water their livestock." (Author unknown)

This writing, by an unknown author, describes for us the affect geography has on history. The writer lists first, and foremost—water. Man cannot survive without water. His physical body requires water, raising crops and cattle require water. Throughout history wars have been fought over water, evidence of the critical need for water as a resource. Settlement occurs where water exists; pathways connecting settlements develop into highways and highways into major trade routes, all necessary for development and survival—all geographical features.

The Bible records for us a history that God deemed important for us to know. This history was lived out in a geographical area known as Mesopotamia. The eastern sphere of Mesopotamia is known also as the Fertile Crescent. Israel, known also as the *Promised Land* because God promised this land to the descendants of Abraham (**Gen. 15:18-21**), is geographically located within the Fertile Crescent. In this study, we will consider the unique geographical features of Israel as well as the climate and seasons of the Promised Land.

When the descendants of Abraham left Egypt, God gave them holy days to observe (**Leviticus 23:1-22:23**). These holy days have agricultural significance. We must seek to understand the climates and seasons of the Promised Land to fully appreciate these observances.

Mesopotamia (eastern sphere) means the land between the rivers in the original Greek language. The region is enclosed by the **Euphrates** and the **Tigris** rivers north of modern Bagdad. The Kurdistan Mountains are bounded on the west and south by the Euphrates, with the Tigris on the east and the **Taurus** to the north. Within the area of these two rivers, there are two smaller rivers—the **Balih** and **Habur**. The low-lying plains reach an altitude of 1,625 feet in some sectors, and then slope gently toward the Persian Gulf, dividing into two steppes—a wet steppe and a dry steppe. A steppe is a vast, open plain of grassland found between the desert and the mountains. The area of the Fertile Crescent—known as the Levant in modern terms—stretches along the Mediterranean coast from the border of Syria through Lebanon, Israel, and to the Red Sea.

CREATION TO MODERN ISRAEL: A Timeline Study

Hand Drawn Map of Israel

We will begin our time on the geography of the Promised Land by drawing a map. The student will need a blank piece of white paper and a pencil.

1. Place your right hand in the center of your paper. Begin on the left side of your index finger drawing a line, go around your thumb, continue down, but do not bend the line in to meet your wrist, instead, draw the line straight to the edge of the paper (Coastline of Israel).
2. To the right of your pinkie, draw an upright oval. Then draw a larger upright oval just below your wrist, remove your hand and draw a squiggly line connecting the ovals (Sea of Galilee, Jordan River, Dead Sea).
3. Draw an arrow with the tip of the arrowhead pointed at the bump your thumb made. The shaft of the arrow should almost reach the squiggly line (Jezreel Valley divides Israel from East to West).
4. Below the arrow (Jezreel Valley) and between the coast and the Jordan River, draw four vertical lines leaving space between, and a little extra space between the second and third lines. Then draw another vertical line to the right of the Sea of Galilee, the Jordan River and the Dead Sea (Geological sections of Israel).
5. Draw a figure eight tipped on its side below the vertical lines (Negev).
6. In the top section of the map, draw four horizontal lines above the arrow (Jezreel Valley).
7. Draw a large box above the horizontal lines outer edges between the coast and the Sea of Galilee (Upper Galilee).
8. Write between the vertical lines: 1.Coastal Plain; 2.Shephelah; 3. Hill Country (Central Range); 4. Wilderness; 5.Jordan Valley; 6. Transjordan (Eastern Range).
9. Between the horizontal lines beneath the Upper Galilee, write Lower Galilee (Dt. 8:7-14).

Routes and Passes

International Coastal Highway/Via Maris

The Coastal Highway (Via Maris) is divided by the river Yarqon known in Hebrew as *Nahal Yarqon* (nahal is a stream or small river). The Sharon Plain is to the north; it is 40 miles long and 10 miles east to west. To the south is the Philistine Plain which is also 40 miles long and 15 miles east to west at its widest point.

Mt. Carmel creates a peninsula which interrupts the otherwise flat Coastal Plain. North of Carmel is the Plain of Asher; it is 25 miles long and 10 miles east to west. The Plain of Dor, mentioned in **Joshua 11:1-3** and **12: 23**, is 20 miles long and 2.5 miles east to west.

Via Maris Coastal Highway

From Al-Qantara, Egypt (which has a connecting route to Heliopolis), the Via Maris Coastal Highway runs to Damascus passing through Sinai Gaza, Ashkelon, Ashdod, Joppa, and Dor. Then, it turns East through Megiddo, Capernaum, and Hazor, crossing the Jordan River at Jacob's Ford, Golan Heights, and Damascus, finally connecting with the King's Highway.

King's Highway

The King's Highway (mentioned in **Num. 21:22**) is no doubt the same highway Abraham used when he was in pursuit of those who had taken Lot captive in **Genesis 14:13-15**. This was a major trade route of antiquity. The route began in Heliopolis, Egypt, crossed to Clysma (Suez) on through the Mitla Pass, to Elath, Aqaba, before turning northward through the Arabah, past Petra, through Kerak (capital of Moab) to Madaba, Rabbah Ammon/Philadelphia-(Bostra). Then, continuing on to Shechem, Hazor, Bostra, Damascus and to Tadmor ending at Resafa on the Upper Euphrates. It is a major north-south route connecting most of the Middle East.

Central Ridge Route

Even though it is known by all these names—i.e. Judean Ridge Route, Way of the Patriarchs, and Watershed Route—I will refer to it as the *Way of the Patriarchs* (or *Judean Ridge Route*). This route runs along the ridge of the Samarian and Judean Hills. It also runs north and south and transverses the land from Shechem, Bethel, Jerusalem, and Hebron to Beersheba.

Beth Horon Ridge Route (BHRR)

The Beth Horon (BHRR) is a continuous hard limestone ridge which ascends from the Plain of Aijalon running through the upper and lower Beth Horon on to the Western Plateau near Gibeon on the Benjamin Plateau—which is the heart of Judea. This gives easy access in all directions: SE to Jerusalem, and E to King's Highway.

Gezer and Jaffo guard this highway into Central Benjamin. Gezer is significant also because of its close proximity to Jabneel; which was located about four miles (6km) from the Mediterranean Sea where the Coastal Highway turns east. Gezer guards both the Via Maris and the BHRR.

Kishon Pass

This pass runs between Mt. Carmel and the Shephelah (Foothills) of Galilee to the Sharon Plain. It separates the Carmel Range from the low-lying hills that stand between the Valley of Jezreel and the Sharon Plain. The southeastern approaches to the Jezreel Valley, on to Beth-Shean, link the Jezreel Valley with routes coming from Transjordan.

Aruna Mountain Pass

Wadi Ara (*Aruna*) is a 20 kilometer wadi that begins in the north of Israel and runs southwest to the Sharon Plains on the coast.

Valleys

Aijalon Valley (AV)

This valley is guarded by Gezer and Lod. It is the western door into CENTRAL BENJAMIN. Aijalon Valley is a broad chalk valley. The *power* that is in control of the valley and the low hills to the north and the south is in command of Jerusalem's first line of defense from the west, as well as the link to the port of Joppa.

Elah Valley

Guarded by Azekah and Socho, the valley is a natural approach to the Hill Country. It was used as a staging area for attacks out onto the coastal plains of Ekron, Gath Azekah, Socho, and Moresheth.

Sorek Valley

There is a *wadi* (dry river bed) that runs from the Judean Hills to the Coastal Plain and offers a natural approach to the Judean Hills. It lies NE of Beth Shemesh (mentioned in **Jud. 14:1, 16:4, 1 Sam. 6:12 and Josh. 15:10**).

Guverian Valley

The Guverian Valley is a chalk depression that separates the hill country of Judah from the Lowlands.

The Promised Land (the land chosen by God for His chosen people) was in fact a battle ground. Within Canaan were the passes of antiquity that connected the two international highways. These highways connected Egypt and the Arabian Peninsula with Mesopotamia. When the great empires to the north or Egypt to the south wanted to expand their borders, the battle would take place in Canaan. God placed His people in a battle ground. Why? In order for the children of Israel to live victoriously and in peace, they needed to live in obedience to Him, for His protection.

Climate and Agriculture

The Promised Land lies between the sea and the desert and is influenced by both. That geographical area has a mixture of mountains, canyons, passes, and plains; it has bodies of water, swamps, and dry, harsh plains. The land is diverse with a range in altitude from 9,000 feet above to 1,300 feet below sea level. This land has double exposure. The Mediterranean basin lies to the west and a desert to the east with the characteristics of desert life. The temperatures vary. In May, the mountain temperatures run in the 80's; in dry areas of the land, the temperatures run into the 100's. Israel proper enjoys a moderate climate throughout the year.

Rains

The *Early Rains,* known also as the Former Rains, arrive in September and run through November. The Early Rains open the agricultural year. The soil is hard since there has been no rain to loosen it up since April. Farmers depend on the early rains to loosen it up so that they can begin their plowing—especially in Biblical times as there was no modern equipment (see **Dt. 11:14, Jer. 5:24, Hos. 6:3, Joel 2:23, and Jas. 5:7**).

The Hard Rains begin in December and run through February (**Song 2:11**).

The Latter Rains come before harvest and summer drought.

Mountains

The *Central Range* receives snow but it generally disappears in a day.

In **2 Samuel 23:20**, there is a reference to the time of the snow. The *Eastern Range* (i.e. Mt. Hermon) is snow-covered most of the year.

Dews

Dews are excessive, and sometimes so heavy, it looks like it rained. Between the months of June, July and August, the dew is equal to seven inches of rain (**1 Ki. 17:1**).

Rainfall

Jerusalem receives up to 26 inches of annual rainfall while Jericho, which lies on the eastern side of the watershed, receives only 6 inches of rain a year. Also, the higher the altitude—the greater the rainfall. In Israel, there is more rainfall in the north than in the south.

"And it shall come to pass, if you shall hearken diligently unto my commandments which I command you this day, to love the Lord your God, and to serve Him with all your heart and with all your soul, that I will give you the rain of your land in his due season, the first rain and the latter rain..." (**Dt. 11:13-14**).

The climate of Israel reveals a *WILL* behind it—man is not in control. The climate is regular enough for methodical labor for a harvest, but the regularity is often interrupted if early rains or latter rains do not come; and often, there can be a drought. Other nations, with the same climate, understood the concept of *WILL* behind their climate. In these other nations, this understanding resulted in human sacrifices and mutilation to appease the gods. The character of Israel's God is moral, the climate was used to punish, warn, and to call to repentance.

"And I also have given you cleanness of teeth in all your cities, and want of bread in all your places: yet have you not returned unto me, saith the Lord. And also I have withheld the rain from you..." (**Amos 4:6-11**).

Winds

The prevailing wind is from the West which blows in off the Mediterranean. In winter, the winds are from the southwest and bring rain (**Lk. 12:54**). During the summer, the winds come from the northwest and bring relief from the heat. Other winds include infrequent and irregular north winds in October which bring dry, cold weather. The East, SE and South winds are hot and bring great discomfort. (For further study see: **Lk. 12:55, Jer. 4:11 and Ezek. 19:12, 27:26**)

Crops

<u>Grapes</u> were harvested as early as July or as late as early September. In antiquity, the last rainfall was in April, and three to five months later, the grapes were harvested. How is it possible in antiquity to reap a harvest when there has been no rain? It is because the dew waters the vines throughout the summer. During the darkness of night through the dry season, the Lord provided the moisture needed for the grapes to come to fruition. Just as He does with each of us—through our long dark, dry seasons, He works to bring the fruit of our obedience to fruition in our lives.

The fruit of the vine was used for wine, juice and raisins. The leaves from the vine are stuffed with rice or meat, and cooked for a dish known as stuffed grape leaves. When pruned and cut back, the dry vines were used for fuel.

<u>Olives</u> were harvested after the first rain. They were used for different grades of oil, in food, and for fuel. Olives were also processed with salt to be consumed.

<u>Figs</u> were used for fig date honey, and were eaten fresh or dried. The pits were used for fodder for the animals, or were burned for charcoal. Grapes, olives and figs, their three principal crops, were traded for wheat.

<u>Wheat</u> was harvested in September. Wheat requires 12 inches of rain, so it was only grown in certain parts of the land. The yield in antiquity was a 5 to 1 ratio. One kernel was for

planting and the 4 fold increase used for food. During the Roman period the yield increased to 10 fold. Understanding this gives us a greater understanding of the tremendous blessing Isaac received from the Lord as recorded in **Genesis 26:12**, *"Then Isaac sowed in the land, and received in the same year a hundredfold; and the Lord blessed him."*

In Egypt, the farmer linked his efforts with the Nile River. The process was purely mechanical and under man's control. Not so in *The Promised Land* where the children of Israel would need to depend on the Lord for the rain in its due season.

> *"For the land, where you go in to possess it, is not as the land of Egypt . . . where you sowed seed and watered it with your foot. . . "* (Dt. 11:10).

The land of promise was, *"A land which the Lord thy God cares for: the eyes of the Lord thy God are always upon it, from the beginning of the year even until the end of the year"* (**Dt. 11:12**).

The children of Israel were instructed to "take heed" and not be deceived into following other gods. The Lord clearly listed for them the blessings of obedience and the curse of disobedience in **Deuteronomy 11:16-17**. In **Deuteronomy 28: 1-14**, the blessings for obedience are listed, followed in verse 15 onward, with a detailed description of the curses for disobedience.

References

Ephraim, S. (Ed.). (1993). *The new encyclopedia of archaeological excavations in the Holy Land.* Jerusalem, IL: The Israel Exploration Society Carta.

Monson, J. M. (1983). *A regional study guide to the land of the Bible.* Rockford, IL: Biblical Backgrounds, Inc.

Monson, J. M. (1983). *Introductory map studies in the land of the Bible.* Rockford, IL: Biblical Backgrounds, Inc.

Smith, G. A. (1894). *The historical geography of the Holy Land.* Jerusalem, IL: Ariel Publishing House.

CHAPTER TWO

CREATION TO THE FALL

DISCUSSION QUESTION: When were Lucifer and the Angels created?

    The Bible holds an historical account of the people and the empires of the ancient Near East and provides a detailed account of the history of God's chosen people. Israel is set in a strategic location. We have looked at the major international highways of antiquity and have noted that the Promised Land lay in between these highways. The passes and roadways that connected these highways ran through Israel. The people, who controlled these routes or important intersections along these routes, had the ability to control the trade in that area.

    Armies were moved along these same routes; therefore, the great empires would have wanted to have them under their control and would wage war to control them. Israel served as a crossroads for these routes and the Bible often mentions activity along these roadways. The routes of ancient Israel were relevant to the security of the nation.

    With the understanding we now have of the geographical location of Israel within the context of the Fertile Crescent, we will look at the political history of Mesopotamia and the land of Israel. Included will be a selective survey of the great powers and their relevance to the developmental aspects of the area—from Abram's arrival in the land until the Babylonian captivity—with special attention given to the impact that the captivity had on the development of Judaism as a religious system. Continuing on with the history of the Second Temple period until the times of Jesus sets the coming of our Lord in historical context. In conclusion, modern Israel, and the impact it had on the development of Palestinian Identity, will be considered as will the Arab Israeli Conflict.

Challenges of Ancient History

Ancient history is sometimes confusing. For any given name or location, there can be numerous spellings, and for any given event there can be various dates. So do not allow that to deter you. Names in antiquity were written using a different alphabet, as is Hebrew and many other languages today. When the names were transliterated, corresponding letters from our alphabet were chosen. Often there were several options. For example, my last name, KARNI, is transliterated from Hebrew. In Hebrew, the letters *cuff*, *resh*, *nun* and *yod* are used. When my husband transliterated his name, he chose the letters K A R N I. He could have just as easily chosen C A R N E Y. So it has been in history, choices have varied in the transliteration of names and places.

Dating

Carbon is a naturally abundant element found in the atmosphere (earth, oceans, and every living creature). C-12 is the most common isotope. Only one in a trillion carbon atoms is C-14. C-14 is produced in the upper atmosphere when nitrogen-14 (N-14) is altered through the effects of cosmic radiation bombardment when a proton is displaced by a neutron (effectively changing the nitrogen atom into a carbon isotope). The new isotope is called radiocarbon because it is radioactive (not dangerous). Radiocarbon is naturally unstable and will spontaneously decay back into N-14. It takes 5,730 years for half a sample of radiocarbon to decay back into nitrogen (another 5,730 for the other half to decay). The period of time it takes for half of the sample to decay is called "half-life".

RADIOCARBON OXIDIZES (or combines with oxygen) and enters the biosphere through natural processes like breathing and eating. Plants and animals naturally incorporate both the abundant C-12 isotope and the much rarer radiocarbon isotope into their tissues in about the same proportions that the two occur in the atmosphere during their lifetimes. When a creature dies, it ceases to consume more radiocarbon while the C-14 that is already in its body continues to decay back into nitrogen.

So, if we find a creature whose C-14 is half of what it is supposed to be (that is one C-14 atom for every two trillion C-12 instead of one in every trillion), we can assume the creature has been dead for about 5,730 years (since half the radiocarbon is missing).

Carbon Dating-The Premise

- The rate of the unstable radioactive C-14 isotope decays into the stable non-radioactive N-14 isotope
- The ratio of C-12 to C-14 found in a given specimen
- And the ratio of C-12 to C-14 found in the atmosphere at the time of the specimen's death

Carbon Dating-The Controversy

Based upon a set of questionable assumptions:

- Assume the rate of decay has remained the same throughout the unobservable past
- Assume the ratio of C-12 to C-14 in the atmosphere has remained constant in the unobservable past
- Dates derived are often wildly inconsistent

Bias of Researchers

For an example of a researcher's bias, we will consider Peter BetBasoo's commentary concerning the Assyrians: "The Assyrians never conquered and destroyed; they conquered and civilized, teaching their subjects the art of the highest civilization then in existence." BetBasoo's is the only scholar I have read who is of this opinion. Another example would be a group of French archeologists hired by a group of Palestinians to disprove that the Children of Israel conquered Jericho as is recorded in the Bible; thereby discrediting the modern Jews claim to an ancient homeland.

New Discoveries

Another influencing factor which can change old ideas is *new discoveries*. For example, the **Hurrians** were viewed as nomads until recent archeological discoveries revealed that they not only lived in cities but they were a highly developed society.

Oopart

OOPART is an acronym which stands for *Out of Place Artifacts*. These are documented artifacts that have been discovered in a stratum that is different from the time in which they are believed to have existed. For example in 1958, Dr. Huerzeler of the Museum of Natural History in Basel, Switzerland, unearthed a human jaw bone at a depth of 600 feet in a coal mine in Tuscany, Italy. The bone had belonged to a child between the ages of five and seven. Though flattened like a sheet of iron, the jaw was declared by several experts to be not only human, but modern-looking at that. But, what mystified them was that it had been encased in a **Miocene** stratum geologically dated at 20 million years.

Dr. Huerzeler declared it to be the world's oldest man, but his fellow anthropologists did not dare give it the same distinction. Here were human remains more modern in appearance than all the "ape-men" forms ever found, yet they were five times as old as any of them. In fact, the jaw bone is as old, if not older, than many ancestors of the apes. The bone raised more problems than answers, so the find was quickly "shelved" and no further work was ever done to give it due recognition.

It is no wonder that the study of ancient history can be confusing. For myself, personally, I have solved any problem of confusion by using the Bible as my standard. It has absolute authority! That is my bias. The ancient history that is recorded in the Bible is chronological, beginning with creation and ending with the promise of the Second Coming of Jesus Christ. The history recorded in the Bible is history with a purpose. It is that history that we will be using to establish a timeline into which we can factor secular history.

Creation

Genesis 1:1, *"In the beginning God created the heavens and the earth."*

- **God Eternal, existing before the universe.**
- *Omnipotent*—invincible (unconquerable), all-powerful.

There is no attempt in this verse to "prove" God's existence. This was recorded when no one doubted God. These are probably the first words ever written down, either by God Himself, or later, revealed to Adam. We will discuss the possibilities of this later.

No other <u>Cosmogony</u>, which is the branch of philosophy dealing with the origin and general structure of the universe, whether in ancient paganism or modern naturalism, even mentions the absolute origin of the universe. All begin with the *space|time|matter universe*, already existing in a primeval state of chaos. They, then, attempt to speculate how it might have "evolved" into the present form. <u>Evolutionists</u> propose that elementary particles of matter evolved out of nothing, then developed through natural forces into complex systems.

<u>Pagan pantheism</u> also begins with elementary matter in various forms evolving into complex systems by the forces of nature personified as different gods and goddesses. But, significantly, the concept of the special creation of the universe of

space and time is found nowhere in any religion or philosophy except in **Genesis 1:1** (Defender's Study Bible, ICR).

Genesis 1:1 appropriately records the creation of space ("the heaven"), of time ("in the beginning"), and of matter ("the earth")—the *tri-universe*—the *space|time|matter* continuum which constitutes our physical cosmos. The Creator of this *tri-universe* is a **triune God**. Elohim ("im") is a plural form meaning more than two. There is a different plural ending in Hebrew for more than two. **Genesis 1:1** is the materialization of Elohim thought. "Bara" means "created out of nothing". This is the only time *bara* is used in the Bible. The First Law of Thermodynamics states that "neither matter nor energy can be created or destroyed" (Defender's Study Bible, ICR).

Gap Theory

Genesis 1:1. This verse, according to the Gap Theory, takes us back to original creation, sometime in the past when God created the heavens and the earth and the host of angelic beings—a time in the past when Lucifer was an intermediary between God and the inhabitants of original earth. Millions or billions of years may have run their course during the first creation; we do not know. Millions or billions of years may have elapsed between verse one and verse two of Genesis. God spoke and materialized the original thought of the divine idea which became the heavens and the earth.

Genesis 1:2, *"The earth was without form and void; and darkness was on the face of the deep."*

This verse is believed to refer to an indefinite interval of time which separates primordial creation from the organization of the terrestrial globe. As the author is about to describe, this interval gives us latitude in explaining the transformations through which matter has undergone according to the various scientific hypotheses (Crampon).

The words translated *"form"* and *"void"* are from the Hebrew words *tohoo* and *bohoo* (**Gen. 1:1**) and are very descriptive. *Tohoo* (8414 Strong's) meaning to lay waste, desolate, in confusion, without form, and *bohoo* (922 Strong's) is an undistinguishable ruin, emptiness.

In **Isaiah 45:18**, God clearly states that He did not create the world *tohoo* and *bohoo* (nor can I imagine that the materialization of the thought of God would be tohoo and bohoo).

According to the Gap Theory, the earth *became* without form and void due to an outbreak of rebellion (i.e. Lucifer and his angels). The state of the earth in verse two was the result of God's judgment. If true, this would have been the FIRST ENVIRONMENTAL CHANGE. It is also conceivable that God allowed Satan to take his rebellion full course and the result was desolation. Just as rebellious man today, if allowed to continue in his destructive course, would render our world void—thankfully Jesus will intervene!

Declaration of War

Just as we find clues in Isaiah in regard to original creation, we find clues in other prophetic books in regard to Lucifer and his angels.

Lucifer

In **Ezekiel 28: 11-19**, we find an interesting record of the king of Tyrus. In **Verse 11** there is a transition: there was no king of Tyrus only a prince spoken of earlier in the chapter. The king of Tyrus is a being above and beyond the sphere of human life, "*Thou sealest up the sum, full of wisdom, and perfect in beauty.*" The tenor of this prophecy indicates that a different personage is in view. This description could not be applied to any human being. The NIV reads: "*. . . You were the model of perfection. . .*"

"*Thou hast been in Eden, the garden of God. . . .*" No one was in Eden, the garden of God, except for Adam, Eve, and Satan. So it must be concluded then that the "king of Tyrus" is none other than Satan. He was personally possessing the body of the "prince of Tyrus" just as he had possessed the body of the "king of Babylon" (Isa. 14:12-15) and the body of Judas (Lk. 22:3). Satan's strategy in first taking over the body of the king of Babylon and then the prince of Tyre (rather than leaving it to lower ranking powers) was probably related to the great military influence developing in Babylon, and the economic influence of Phoenicia. By controlling the leaders of these two world powers, he could largely control the world.

". . . *In the day that thou wast created. . .* " –*created* not born. This statement could not have been true of an earthly king of Tyre. "*Thou art the anointed cherub that covereth. . .* " (v. 14). In other words, the anointed cherub on God's Holy Mountain (covering the Garden of Eden)—the highest of all of God's created angels is—Satan.

Lucifer was in an exalted state as is further demonstrated in that: music surrounded him from the day of his creation, he was protected by mineral beauty, and he had never known a lesser state from the day of his creation. Only the throne of God was higher than he. He was set in the government of God to be a ruler over creation. He was the anointed cherub (covering, protecting with spread out wings), a priestly role associated with worship (Rev. 4:9, 10: 5 and 11:14).

He was "*...perfect... ...until iniquity was found in thee*" (v.15). When iniquity was found in Lucifer (Light Bearer), he became Satan (The Adversary).

"*Thou hast defiled thy sanctuaries... ...I will bring thee to ashes upon the earth in the sight of all of them that behold thee*" (v. 18). Some scholars believe that Satan received worship from beneath—from the inhabitants of earth, and offered to God above. (This will be discussed later.)

" . . .*take up this proverb against the king of Babylon. . .* " (Isa. 14:4).

Although this prophecy is directed at the earthly king of Babylon, it goes far beyond him (as we will read in the following verses) to the wicked spirit possessing his body and inspiring his actions—just as Satan possessed and used the serpent in the Garden, etc. "*...How art thou fallen from heaven, O Lucifer...*" (Isa. 14:12).

Formal Declaration of War

1. I will ascend into heaven (v. 13).
2. I will exalt my throne above the stars of God (v. 14); stars are angels.
3. I will also sit on the mount of the congregation on the farthest sides of the north (v. 13).
4. I will ascend above the heights of the clouds (v. 14).
5. I will be like the Most High (v. 14).

Some scholars believe that the rebellion began on earth in the heart of Lucifer and the inhabitants of earth along with some angels who chose to follow Satan. They believe that the inhabitants of earth scattered and are now the demons that plaque the earth (angels, archangels, principalities, powers, seraphim, cherubs of all these orders of creation). Lucifer was the climax in gifts, power and beauty. He was so high-ranking that even Michael dared not bring accusations against him (Jude 9).

This is the *Gap Theory*. All this took place between **Genesis 1:1** and **Genesis 1:2** with the reconstruction of earth beginning in verse two (The Invisible War). Now we will look at the **opponents** of the Gap Theory.

The opponents of the Gap Theory argue that this theory requires a worldwide cataclysm (God's judgment) at the end of the geological ages (when Lucifer rebelled) in order to account for the globally inundated and darkened earth (*tohoo* and *bohoo*) described in **Genesis 1:2**. The Gap Theory (its opponents believe) is self-defeating geologically. The geological age system is based entirely on the *Principal of Uniformitarianism*: a geological doctrine that "**processes**", acting in the same manner as at present and over a long span of time, are sufficient to account for all current geological features and all past geological changes—a premise which precludes any such worldwide cataclysm, and requires the interpreting of earth history by the extrapolation of present slow geological *processes* into the remote past (Defender's Bible). The concept of the *geological ages* is based entirely on a uniformitarian explanation of the fossil beds and sedimentary rocks of the earth's crust, which would all have been destroyed by the pre-Adamic cataclysm.

"*Thou hast been in Eden the garden of God; every precious stone was thy covering, the sardius, topaz, and the diamond, the beryl, the onyx, and the jasper, the sapphire, the emerald, and the carbuncle, and gold...*" (Ezek. 28:13).

It is believed by the opponents of the Gap Theory that the Garden of Eden (that Lucifer was in) was in the *heavens*. Ezekiel 28: 13 emphasizes precious stones, which is quite different from the earthly Eden which was prepared by God as a terrestrial model of His own Eden in heaven. Lucifer was in a Garden of Eden that was a place of rare mineral beauty—the New Jerusalem (**Rev.** 21:19-20). (Institute for Creation Research).

TIMELINE ENTRY		
Genesis 1-3	Genesis 4	Genesis 5
Lucifer-Angels	Cities, Bronze and Iron	God's Plan
Man/Fall	Musical instruments	for man
Environmental	Farming (cattle)	
change	vegetarians	

Genesis 1:2-5: The measurement of time is from evening to morning. In Judaism, the day begins and ends with the sunset, so the Jewish Sabbath begins at sundown on Friday and ends at sundown on Saturday. The early believers were Jewish. They continued to attend the House of Prayer on Shabbath (Saturday when the Shabbath ended). Saturday evening, they would gather together to discuss the scriptures read that day at the service. Sunday was a work day, so they would have met together on Saturday evening which was the evening of the first day.

Genesis 2:4: Generations (*toledoth*) is the first occurrence of the formula which marks the key subdivisions of the book, "These are the generations of..." In all the other *toledoth's*, the name of a specific patriarch is attached. Parallels with the terminology of the ancient Babylonian tablets indicate that these names are actually the signatures of the original writers of the particular tablets. Each of the patriarchs kept a narrative record of his generations and then appending his name at the end when he was ready to turn them over to the next in line. God Himself either wrote this section directly or specifically revealed it to Adam. (ICR)

Mitochondrial Eve

Genesis 2:7: Man was formed from the elements of the earth (Gen. 2:18, 21-22).

Eve was created from Adam's rib. DNA research in 1987, across all of today's major racial groups concluded that every person on earth today can trace their heritage back to a single common female ancestor.

The Garden

Genesis 3:1: The Serpent is understood by all scholars to be Lucifer. He challenges God's word, and His goodness.

Genesis 3:6: The entrance of a second will is introduced. One of the differences between eternity and time is that in eternity there is only one will.

Genesis 3:16: "*... greatly multiply thy sorrow in conception...*" (KJV). "*... greatly increase your pains in childbearing...*" (NIV). Were there children born in the Garden? It is a possibility, but it is an unknown factor. Science uses the term of unknown factor when they are unable to explain something due to missing information. As Christians, we should never be afraid to admit when we don't know the answer to something such as "where did Cain get his wife?" That is an unknown factor. We need to emphasize what we do know—that Jesus died for us to give us eternal life. And if the question about Cain remains important in eternity, it will be answered.

Genesis 3:17: "... *cursed is the ground (adamah) for thy sake...*". The very elements out of which all things were made were included in the curse, so that the *whole creation* (**Rom.** 8:22) was brought under bondage to a universal principal of "corruption" –literally *decay* (**Rom.** 8:21). All things had been built up by God from the basic elements of matter, but now they would all begin to decay (Note: *cosmos* may relate to the prior sin of the angelic host of heaven. ICR)

Genesis 3:18: "... *thorns and thistles...* " There was an environmental change. The beneficent structures began to deteriorate in varying degrees. <u>The Second Law of Thermodynamics</u> states that the universal tendency for systems to decay proceeds irreversibly toward ultimate equilibrium and cessation of all processes (ICR).

Genesis 4:16-24: Nod was most probably the name of a region in which Cain wandered (*nod* means wandering). The first city recorded is "Enoch" which means *dedicated*—as in ushering in something new.

>Cities
>Brass and Iron
>Harp and Organ (sense of breathing; a reed instrument)
>Farming/Vegetarians

Genesis 5:1a is Adam's signature at the conclusion. Genesis 5:1b is the opening statement of Noah's record. (ICR)

Genesis 5
God's Plan for Man:

<u>ADAM</u> = Hebrew root *man, red earth, blood*
<u>SETH</u> = SUBSTITUTE (105=Enos) (912)
<u>ENOS</u> = MORTAL/HUMANITY (90=Cainan) (905)
<u>CAINAN</u> = ACQUISITION/PURCHASED
　　　(70=Mahalaleel) (910)
<u>MAHALALEEL</u>= SPLENDOR OF GOD (65=Jared) (895)
<u>JARED</u> = DESCEND (162=Enoch) (962) **HOLY SPIRIT**

ENOCH = DEDICATED/USHERED IN NEW
(65=Methuselah) (365)
METHUSELAH = DEATH TO SEND (187=Lamech)
(969)
LAMECH = UNUSED ROOT, CONQUEROR/KING
(182=Noah) (777)
NOAH = REST (600 years old when flood came)
Jared=Holy Spirit
Enoch=Rapture
Methuselah=Tribulation   187 when Lamech born
Lamech=Second Coming   182 when Noah born
Noah=Millennial reign   600 when floods came
                               (Gen. 7:6)

Methuselah was 969 when he died in the year the floods came. He lived longer than any other human being—a testament to God's grace and mercy.

႘

References

Barnhouse, D. G. (1965). *The invisible war.* Grand Rapids, MI: Zondervan Publishing House.

Gish, D. T. (1979). *Evolution? The fossils say no!* Green Forrest, AR: Master Books.

Institute for Creation Research Scientists and Scholars (10). (2013). *Creation basics and beyond.* Dallas, TX: ICR Publishing.

Morris, H. M. (Notes and appendixes). (1995). *The defender's study bible.* Grand Rapids, MI: World Publishing.

Schaffer, F. A. (1972). *Genesis in space and time.* Carol Stream, IL: Tyndale house Publishers Inc.

Schaffer, F. A. (1972). *He is there and He is not silent.* Downers Grove, IL: Intervarsity Press.

Tregelles, S. P. (1949). *Hebrew and Chaldee Lexicon.* Grand Rapids, MI: Wm. B. Eerdmans Publishing Company.

CHAPTER THREE

FLOOD TO SHECHEM

DISCUSSION QUESTION: Who were the Sons of God in Genesis 6?

Sons of God and the Daughters of Man

In Genesis six we encounter an interesting account which has scholars divided. The Hebrew phrase "bene elohim", found in Genesis 6:1-7 and translated into English as "...sons of God..." is believed by some scholars to refer to angelic beings. This was the uniform interpretation of the Jews, who translated the phrase as "angels of God" in their Septuagint translation of the Old Testament (The Truth About Angels by Terry Law). However, there are some of the opinion that the phrase refers to something other than angels.

In the following three parallel usages, the contextual meaning of *bene elohim* seems to be something other than angels, which are also called morning stars. For example, in verse seven of chapter thirty-eight, the "morning stars" (which are angels) are listed separate from the "sons of God".

- Job 1:6: *Now there came a day when the sons of God came to present themselves before the Lord and Satan came along among them.*
- Job 2:1: *Again there was a day when the sons of God came to present themselves before the Lord, and Sa-*

tan came among them to present himself before the Lord.
- **Job 38:7**: *When the morning stars sang together, and all the sons of God shouted for joy.*

Morning stars are also angels (scriptures below) who followed Satan in rebellion and were cast down, bound, and held in darkness until the Day of Judgment. If they are chained, how could they be wandering the earth taking wives from the daughters of man? And who were the *"bene elohim, sons of God"*?

- **Revelation 12:9**: *And that great dragon was cast out...he was cast out into the earth, and his angels were cast out with him.*
- **2 Peter 2:4**: *For if God spared not the angels that sinned but cast them down to hell, and delivered them into chains of darkness, to be reserved unto judgment...*
- **Jude 6**: *And the angels which kept not their first estate, but left their own habitation, He has reserved in everlasting chains under darkness unto the judgment of the great day.*

Scholars, who favor the Gap Theory, believe the sons of God were the inhabitants of original earth. Satan is believed to have represented God to these inhabitants and to take their praise and worship to the throne of God. They further believe that these inhabitants followed Lucifer in his rebellion and as a result of this rebellion, they were disembodied and scattered throughout the world, becoming the evil spirits that roam the earth today and in the days of Noah (**The Invisible War** by Barnhouse).

Whichever theory one subscribes to, the intent of the writer of **Genesis 6** (probably Noah) was clearly that of introducing a monstrous eruption of demonic forces on earth leading to universal corruption and eventual judgment (ICR).

Continuing on in **Genesis 6: 2**, we read that these beings "*... took them wives...*" In rebuttal to the theory that these are fallen angels, the verse in **Matthew 22:30** is used. It reads "*. . . they neither marry nor are given in marriage, but are as the angels of God in heaven.*" The opinion being that the angels who do not marry are in heaven. Those who are not supporters of the Gap Theory believe that some fallen angels took on the body and functions of man, including sex. This was probably an attempt by Satan to corrupt all flesh and thereby thwart the coming of God's promised Seed.

The word translated "giants" in **Genesis 6:4** is *Nephilim*. In the Hebrew, this word shares the same root as the word "fall" and leads some scholars to believe that the more suitable interpretation would be the "fallen ones". In that case, "fallen ones" is a name that would refer not only to their parents, but would also refer to their physical bodies. In **Numbers 13:33**, the same word is used in connection with giants in Canaan at the time of Joshua. The giants were also known as *Anakim*, the sons of *Anak*. Whichever interpretation you accept, this unorthodox union resulted in giants and "*. . . the wickedness of man was great . . . every imagination of the thoughts of his heart was only evil continually*" (**Gen. 6:5**). Noah and his family were possibly the only humans who were not genetically altered through sexual relations with *bene elohim*, or who had not yielded their bodies to demon possession. In **Genesis 6:9**, the word *tawmeem* (perfect) means entire or without blemish, and is a word that would be used for an animal suitable for sacrifice. In other words, Noah was not genetically polluted!

The Lord's heart concerning the state of man is reflected in **Genesis 6:7** "*. . . I will destroy man. . .*" "*. . . for it repenteth me that I have made them.*" The word *repenteth* is translated from the Hebrew word *Nacham* which means to breathe heavily as in sorrow. This is an indication of the broken heart of God.

Noah's signature, concluding his personal record, is found in **Genesis 6:9**. In **Genesis 5:1b**, we find Noah's opening statement of his *toledoth*. **Verse 9b** is the first sentence of the *toledoth* written by Noah's sons.

The Flood: Second Environmental Change

During the flood, subterranean water chambers that were under a great deal of pressure would have been breached. This would have resulted in an enormous amount of carbon 12 being released into the oceans and atmosphere. The water in these subterranean chambers would not have contained carbon 14, as the water was shielded from cosmic radiation. This would upset the ratio of carbon 14 to carbon 12. (14 would decrease). There was a climate change and the atmosphere no longer was tropical with a canopy (ICR).

Genesis 6-10

There exists a multitude of evidence for a worldwide flood in the collective memory legends. Dr. Aaron Smith of the University of Greensboro in North Carolina has collected 80,000 works in 72 languages that mention a global flood; about 70,000 of them mention an Ark. The Gilgamesh Epic is probably the most well-known legend of the flood. Also, recent discoveries in plate tectonics and crustal physics have shown a much flatter earth could easily have been flooded, with the resultant volcanic and geologic activity altering the land surface.

After the flood, the dietary needs for man changed and humans were given divine permission to eat animal flesh. There was a greater need for animal protein in view of the nutrient impoverished soils of the post-diluvium world and the much more rigorous climatic conditions. However, they are instructed, *"But the flesh with the life thereof, which is the blood thereof, shall you not eat"* **(Gen. 9:4).** God clearly states that life is in the blood. With that in mind, consider what the cost of rebellion was. What price had to be paid? Was it not life (the blood of Jesus)?

Table of Nations

Genesis 10

In verse one of Genesis 10, we find the third toledoth, presumably marking the signatures of Shem, Ham and Japheth after completing their narrative of the Flood and the immediate Post-Flood years. This marks the end of the first and only authentic account of the great Flood. Japheth, after completing the narrative of the flood, turned the task over to Shem.

Tarshish (10:4) became associated with the **Phoenicians** and their cities of Carthage and Tartesons. The early settlers of these cities were the Japhethites who were later conquered by the Phoenicians.

Cush,-also spelled Kish = **Ethiopia (10:6)**
Mizraim = Egypt **(10:6)**
Phut = Libya **(10:6)**
Canaan = Canaanites **(10:6)**
Nimrod = Babylon **(10:8-10)**
Plain of Shinar:
    Babel
    Erech
    Accad (100 miles south of Babylon home of
        Gilgamesh)
    Calneh
    Asshur = Assyria **(10:11)**
    Nineveh = capital of Assyria **(10:11)**

Caphtorim = Philistines **(10:14)**: the most recent archeological discoveries indicate that the Philistines originated in the area of modern Turkey near the Iraq border. The Caphtorim, known today as Palestinians, arrived along the coast of Israel during the same time that Abram arrived in the land **(Gen. 21:32)**
Sidon = Phoenician city **(10:15)**
Heth = Hittites **(10:15)**

> Elam = **Elamites (10:22)**: merged with the Medes to become the Medo-Persia empire
> Aram = **Aramaeans (10:22)**: Aramaic language, portions of the Old Testament were first written in Aramaic

The division of the nations is recorded in **Genesis 10:32, 11:1-2** "... *by these were the nations divided in the earth...* " (10:32). There are 70 nations listed by Shem. These 70 nations were the progenitors of all other nations (not to be interpreted as race which is an evolutionary idea). The record continues "... *they found a plain in the land of Shinar and there they dwelt*" (11:2). Nimrod was the leader of the population at this time (10:9). In **Genesis 11:3**, a brick making industry seems to have been in operation and productive enough that a massive tower project was undertaken (11:4).

Division of Languages

Communication was simple as "... *the whole earth was of one language, and of one speech...* " when man united to build this tower (**Gen. 11:1**). In response to this united effort, God chose to... *confound their language...* " (11:7). In some inexplicable way, God altered the *brain/nerve/speech* giving each family unit (possibly the 70) its own distinctive vocabulary. It is probable that all the families, except Nimrod, departed from Babel around this time.

Babel is also known in history as Sumer. The Sumerians are known in their early history as Ubaidians. The language of the Ubaidians was a *Language Isolate*. A *language isolate* is a natural language with no demonstrable genealogical (genetic) relationship with other languages. The Ubaidians settled in the region known as Sumer (Babel). Their language is the earliest known language discovered through anthropological and archeological discoveries.

In other words, the earliest known language is not related to any other known language, past or present. This is a strong indication that their civilization existed prior to the Tower of Babel and is strongly support for the record of the division of languages recorded in Genesis. In addition, because God had altered the brain, giving each family unit its own distinctive vocabulary, they would have needed to develop a new alphabet to write their new language.

Genesis 11:10 marks the end of Shem's tablet; in **Genesis 10:31**, Shem took over the task of writing his family records which are known as the "Table of Nations". He is now turning the task over to Terah (11:27). As the people scattered, each family gradually became a tribal unit. They all had known how to write, but now with a completely new speech, each tribe would need to invent an entirely new written language.

> Timeline: Above the line, you may write Ubaidians Language Isolate 5000 BC and below the line, the Flood and Tower of Babel with scripture references.

Mesopotamia and the UR of Chaldees

As has been discussed previously (**Genesis 11:10**), man has basic needs for survival—water and communication (including roads) and the ability to grow crops—and these needs dictate where communities will develop. Throughout the history of man, wars have been fought over water rights, roads and passes, and fertile land. In our future study, we will be observing this phenomenon and how it has molded history.

Sumer-Akkad

In 4750 BC (secular dating), the first temple of Ashur was built, also spelled Asur or Assur. Several centuries later, Semites from Syria and Arabian deserts began to infiltrate that area. In the early history of Sumer, tribes were divided against tribes, then city against city. In addition to the wars among the city-states, there were the invasions of barbarians from the east and west. Communities needed to defend themselves and be in a constant state of preparedness.

> Timeline: (above line) 4750 BC, 1ˢᵗ temple to Ashur-Semites infiltrate-Concept of king/lugal.

Concept of King Develops

The elders appointed a *lugal* (big man/strong man) as their military leader of men of arms. Wars began to last longer, and the lugals were able to extend-their authority. The lugals began to appoint their successors, and thus, the concept of a *monarchy* was developed. The lugals took care of the priests who then decreed that the lugals ruled by divine right. Both the lugals and the priests were political positions. The *lugal* is where the concept of king was derived. The king was a warrior who protected the people and led them into battles. So, when the children of Israel demanded a king, they were in fact saying, "We want a mighty warrior to defend and protect us."

The Lord had established a system for judges to settle disputes and priests to deal with worship. Samuel was both a judge and a priest. A judge would have been responsible to settle differences between the people. There were also judges who led Israel in battle. Most of the judges had authority in a local area. There were a few who are known as great judges, and they led Israel in victories. Yet, a judge's authority and influence was more local, whereas, a king's authority would be national. At the time of the judges there were many problems in the fledgling country of Israel: ". . . In those days there was no king in Israel; every man did what was right in his own eyes" (Jud. 21:25). The line of priests was also rebellious and corrupt. In 1 Samuel 2:22, the record of the sons of Eli offers a sad commentary. And in 1 Samuel 8:3, we read of Samuel's sons: *"And his sons walked not in his ways, but turned aside for lucre, and took bribes, and perverted judgment. . . "*, No small wonder that the population demanded a change in administration. *". . . all the elders of Israel gathered to Samuel: ". . . now make us a king to judge us like all the nations"* (**1 Sam. 8:4**).

In the remaining verses of this chapter, Samuel warned the children of Israel what would happen if they insisted on having a king. But the priests, Eli's sons, were corrupt and exploited the people. They misrepresented God to the people. The congregation of Israel was judging God by man, and it was a mistake (1 Sam. 2:22).

In **Deuteronomy 17:14-20**, the Lord Himself warned, *"When thou art come into the land which the Lord your God giveth three, and possess it and dwell in it, and say I will set a king over me, like all other nations that are about me"* —in the preceding verses, the Lord explains to them what a king will require and warns them of the hardships they would endure under the reign of a king. This warning was given before the children of Israel entered the land. Once in the land, the Lord was faithful as is recorded in (I Sam. 12:11), *". . . And the Lord sent Jerubbaal, and Bedan, and Jephthah, and Samuel, and delivered you out of the hand of your enemies on every side and you dwelled safely"*. Yet, they persisted in their desire for a king. "And when you saw that Nahash the king of the children of Ammon came against you, you said unto me, Nay, but a king shall reign over us: when the Lord your God was your king" (**1 Sam. 12:12**). Although the Lord had been faithful to deliver them from their enemies (using the system He established of Judges and Priests), the children of Israel preferred to trust in their own understanding and rejected the Lord as their protector.

> Timeline: (above line) 4750 BC, 1ˢᵗ temple to Ashur-Semites infiltrate-Concept of king/lugal

The first Sumerian king of historic record was **Etana** (also spelled **Eannatune**), the king of **Kish**, and also known as Lagash (2800 BC). Fighting **Umma** over water, he later conquered **Ur** and made himself king of all **Sumer**. The **war of water** between Sumer and Ur continued until it was settled by digging a canal from the Tigris to Lagash. The **Shatt-el-Hai** is still in use and known as the Hai River, or the Gharraf Canal. Sumerian power declined and the Semitic ruler **Saragon I** conquered the entire country (Water).

> Timeline: (above) 2800BC 1st war over water- Saragon I 2300BC trade routes protected

Akkadians (2300BC)

Saragon was from Akkad. His military campaigns were started in the north in a response to an appeal from merchants to keep the trade route open. Traders needed to be protected from highwaymen and mountain tribes. As king with a central government, Saragon had the route policed thereby keeping them open and safe.

After conquering Sumer, he went through Persia to the shores of the Mediterranean and north to Asia Minor, possibly all the way to Cyprus. This represents the *first world empire.* The land of Sumer acquired the composite name of Akkad and the people became known ethnically and linguistically as Akkadians. **Aramaic** was known as the official language alongside Akkadian.

Ur-Namma (2112BC -2095BC - 3rd dynasty of Ur): He built a temple to the moon god at Ur. This was the golden age for Sumer—there was unity and peace. But the fertility of the fields was declining due to salt residues, so crop production dwindled, and the surplus of food was depleted. Around 2000BC, there was **The Great Migration** attributed to the need for fertile farmlands.

> Timeline: (above) 2112BC UR dynasty-1st World Empire- Temple to moon god-language Aramaic-2000BC Great Migration

Abram

Abram was from the city of **Ur** (Gen. 11: **28, 31**). The name *Abram* (Abu ramu) means Honored Father, and occurs in lists and contract tablets dating 677 BC, thus demonstrating that Abram was a Babylonian name in use long before and after the time of the Patriarch. His father moved from Ur to Haran, from the old center of the Moon-cult to the new center.

In Canaan, Abraham remained within the sphere of the Babylonian language and influence and most probably the authority. When passing into Egypt, he remained under Semitic rule because the Hyksos were in rule there.

> Timeline: (below) Abram-Shechem-Biblical references

Please Note: By now, students should have an understanding of how to develop the timeline; therefore, this will be the last example.

Dating Abram's Arrival

Many scholars date Abram's arrival in the land between 1900-1720BC. These dates are calculated as follows:
- Abram was 75 years old when he left Haran.
- Abram was 100 years old when Isaac was born.
- Isaac was 60 years old when Jacob was born.
- Jacob was 130 years old when he stood before the Pharaoh of Egypt (Gen. 47:9).

Therefore,

      25 (add this to Abraham; 75 when he left Haran and 100 when Isaac was born)
      60 (Isaac when Jacob was born)
      <u>130</u> (when Jacob went before the Pharaoh)
Total = 215 (years from Abraham's arrival in the land until Jacob leaves)

The Children of Israel were in Egypt for 430 years (1 Ki. 6:1): four hundred and eighty years (480) after the exodus from Egypt, in the fourth year of Solomon's reign which is calculated to be 961 BC—hence dating the Exodus at **1441 BC**. By these calculations, Abraham was born in 2161 BC and entered the land at 2086 BC.

Notably, scholars have widely different opinions on dating historical events. There are scholars who prefer the Exodus to have occurred at 1290 BC, and place Abram's birth at 2010 BC. This would establish the entrance into the land at 1935 BC.

There is yet another that dates Abram's birth at 1795 BC and the entrance into the land at 1720 BC.

It is, therefore, within the realm of possibility that Abraham was born approximately 54 years into the first world empire of Akkad. He may have left in the early part of the Ur dynasty or he could have left around the time the Amorites invaded.

Recent discovery: Tell Khaiber was unearthed by the University of Manchester on March 31, 2013. Tell Khaiber is located about 12 miles from Tell Mugheir (Tell el-Muqayyar), which is the site of ancient Ur. Tell Khaiber is probably around 4000 years old, and is believed to have served as an administrative center for Ur around the time of Abraham.

Amorites – 1900—2000 BC)

As we continue with the historical context of the Fertile Crescent, the next invasion of significance was that of the Amorites. The name Amorite refers to a Semitic-speaking people from ancient Syria who also occupied large parts of Mesopotamia from the 21st century BC. The term Amurru, in Akkadian and Sumerian texts, refers to them as well as to their principal deity.

Origins

In the earliest Sumerian sources beginning in 2400 BC, the land of the Amorites is not associated with Mesopotamia but with the lands immediately to the West, including what is known today as Syria and Israel. They appear as nomadic people in Mesopotamian sources, and they are especially connected with the mountainous region of Jebel Bishri in Syria called the "mountain of the Amorites". A severe drought is believed to be what triggered their migration to southern Mesopotamia. They were one of the instruments in the downfall of the Sumerian Third Dynasty of Ur. The Amorites acquired many powerful kingdoms, and are responsible for the founding of Babylon as a state. They usurped the thrones of the Sumero-

Akkadian states of Isin, Larsa and Kish, culminating in the triumph under **Hammurabi** of **Babylon**.

Effects on Mesopotamia

The rise of the Amorite kingdoms in Mesopotamia brought about deep and lasting repercussions in its political, social, and economic structure, especially in Mesopotamia. The division into kingdoms replaced the Sumero-Akkadian city state in southern Mesopotamia. Men, land, and cattle ceased to belong physically to the gods or to the temples and the king. The new monarchs gave, or let out for an indefinite period, numerous parcels of royal or sacerdotal land, freed the inhabitants of several cities from taxes and forced labor, and seemed to have encouraged a new society to emerge, a society of big farmers, free citizens, and enterprising merchants which was to last throughout the ages. The priests assumed the service of the gods, and cared for the welfare of his subjects, but the economic life of the country was no longer exclusively in their hands. The era of the Amorite kingdoms (2000-1595 BC) is sometimes known as the "Amorite period" in Mesopotamia history.

Alternative View

The Amorites invaded bringing disorder and confusion. The Amorites were
Semitic nomads; they came from the desert to the west of Sumer and Akkad. They gradually became masters of the important cities of Isin and Larsa, resulting in disorder and confusion. This widespread political disorder encouraged the Elamites to attack Ur and to take into captivity its last ruler.

Amorite Father

"*And the word of the Lord came unto me saying, Son of man, cause Jerusalem to know her abominations. And say, thus saith the Lord God unto Jerusalem; thy birth and thy nativity is of the land of Canaan; thy father was an Amorite, and thy mother an Hittite*" (Ezek. 16:3).

Both Amorites and Hittites were present in Canaan when Abram arrived. Abram was a descendant of Shem and the Amorites were descendants from Ham. This is a reference to the influences of these pagans on the children of Israel.

Elamites Conquer

The capital of the Elamites was Susa. They spoke an agglutinative language not related to Sumerian, Semitic, or Indo-European. They destroyed Ur and exerted a great influence over the rulers of Babylonia. After 3000BC, the Elamites were influenced by the Sumerians' system of writing.

Shechem

Abram steps onto the pages of history and enters the land of promise. His first stop is at Shechem. In addition to the significant geographical location of Shechem, it has a historical/spiritual relevance for the nation of Israel. Shechem is the first place that Abram comes to as he obeys God and follows Him to "the land that I will show you" (**Gen. 12:1**). It is on this geographical location that the history of the children of Israel begins.

Shechem, a city in central Israel, becomes a city of great importance in the history of Israel. It is located in the hill country of Ephraim, and because of its location in the middle of the country, it became an important crossroads. The route, the Way of the Patriarchs (Judean Ridge Route) ran from Shechem to Hebron passing through Shiloh, Bethel, Ai, Ramah, Gibeah, Jerusalem and Bethlehem.

The crossroads through Shechem led to both of the international highways of antiquity. The first route (mentioned above), the Way of the Patriarchs (Judean Ridge Route) ran south descending to the Sharon Plain and connected with the Via Maris (International Coastal Highway). The other route ran northeast and then descended east to the Jordan Valley, passing through the Jabbok Valley and ultimately connected with the Kings Highway (Transjordan Highway).

Abram was called by God to leave his country, his kindred, and his father's house (**Gen. 12:1**). We know however that Abram did not begin his relationship with the Lord in complete obedience. In (**Gen. 11:27-32**), the genealogy of Abram's family is recorded through his father Terah. As is the literary style of the Bible that which is of lesser importance is presented first to give context to what is of greater importance—in this case, Abram and the call of God. In **verse 31** of this genealogical record, it is recorded that Abram left Ur of Chaldees to go to the land of Canaan with all his family and they lived in Haran until Abram's father Terah died. Abram then continued on, taking with him his nephew Lot. So, upon arriving in Shechem, the Lord appears to Abram and reaffirms His promise, and Abram built an altar unto the Lord. Then, he left Shechem and traveled to Bethel, which is on the Way of the Patriarchs. Along this route is where Abram spent most of his life.

Jacob

Jacob, returning from Padan-Aram, traveled through the Jabbok Valley, crossed the Jordan River, camped at Succoth and then ascended to Shechem. Here Jacob (renamed Israel) built an altar and named it El-Elohe-Israel, meaning *God, the God of Israel* (**Gen. 33:17-20**). He also dug a well which remains to this day. I have personally visited and drunk from Jacob's well.

After meeting his brother Esau, Jacob moved to Shechem and bought a parcel of land. While living in Shechem, Jacob's daughter Dinah was defiled. The sons of Jacob sought vengeance on the men of Shechem resulting in Jacob moving to Bethel (**Gen. 34**).

Jacob's sons kept their flocks in Shechem and Joseph was sent from Hebron to check on them. Joseph would have traveled the Way of the Patriarchs (Judean Ridge Route) to Shechem (**Gen. 37:12-17**).

Moses

God commanded Moses to enter the Promised Land and go to Shechem to pronounce the blessings for obedience and the curses for disobedience (Dt. 27). Joshua did this when they entered the land. He divided the nation in half. One half stood on Mount Gerizim and the other half stood on Mount Ebal. From Mount Ebal, they shouted the curses for disobedience and from Mount Gerizim they shouted the blessings for obedience.

Joshua

Joshua built an altar on Mount Ebal, and wrote a copy of the law in stone (Josh. 8:30-35). At the end of the conquest, Joshua once again gathered all the people at Shechem and reminded them of the pledge they had made to the Lord. This time Joshua set up a *stone of witness* in Shechem, to be a witness in the event the people denied God (Josh. 24:1-24).

Joseph

The bones of Joseph which were carried from Egypt were buried at Shechem on the land that Jacob had bought (Josh. 24:32). Shechem became one of the cities of refuge (Josh. 20:7, 21:21 and 1 Chr. 6:67).

Abimelech

Abimelech proclaimed himself to be king of Shechem, and at his coronation, Jotham, his younger brother, climbed Mount Gerizim and shouted a curse on Shechem. The city was later destroyed by Abimelech in fulfillment of that curse (Jud. 9:6-49).

Rehoboam-Jeroboam

Rehoboam, son of Solomon, was made king of Israel at Shechem and it was at Shechem that the nation was divided. Jeroboam became king of Israel and Rehoboam reigned as king of Judah. Jeroboam made Shechem the capital of the northern kingdom (1 Ki. 12:1-25). The Samaritans worshipped on

Mount Gerizim and Jesus met with the Samaritan woman at Jacob's well in Shechem (Jn. 4:20).

Samaria

Throughout the history of Israel, Shechem had an important spiritual significance. From the time Abram built an altar unto the Lord God until the time of the captivity of the ten northern tribes, Shechem had served as a place of worship, and a place of commitment to keep the law. Later, it became a place of division and the capital of the Northern Kingdom. After the destruction of the Northern Kingdom, it was repopulated by Assyria with peoples from other conquered countries who then became known as the Samaritans.

Woman at the Well

Jesus knew the history of Shechem. He knew this was the first place Abram came to when he entered the land. He was aware that God had instructed Moses to go to Shechem when they entered the land. He knew of the commitment His people had made at Shechem, and He knew from whence the Samaritans came and why they chose to worship on Mount Gerizim. As He sat by Jacob's well that day, waiting for the divine appointment with the Samaritan woman, I am sure the history of Shechem was on His mind. Of course, God knew before time began that Abram would build an altar there and that one day a needy Samaritan woman would meet her Savior at Jacob's well.

REFEERENCES

Aharoni, Y. & Yonah, M. A. (1977). *The Macmillan Bible Atlas*. New York, NY: Macmillan.

Andersen, H.G. (1975-1976). *The Zondervan pictorial encyclopedia of the Bible*. Grand Rapids, MI: Zondervan.

Balsiger, D. (1976). *In search of Noah's Ark*. Vancouver, BC: Sun Classic Books.

Harrison, R. K. (Ed.). (1988). *The new Unger's Bible dictionary*. Chicago, IL: Moody Press.

Law, T. (2006). *The truth about angels*. Lake Mary, FL: Charisma Media.

Morris, M. & Litt. D. (1995). *The defender's study bible*. Grand Rapids, MI: World Publishing.

Sarel, B. (1997). *Understanding the Old Testament: An introductory atlas to the Hebrew Bible*. Jerusalem, IL: Carta, Jerusalem.

Snell, D. C. (1997). *Life in the Ancient Near East 310-332 BCE*. New Haven, CT: Yale University Press.

Stiles II, D. Shechem. waynestiles@dcc-smots.org.

Strong, J. (1947). *Strong's exhaustive concordance*. Nashville, TN: Thomas Nelson Publishers.

Tregelles, S. P. (1949). *Hebrew and Chaldee Lexicon*. Grand Rapids, MI: Wm. B. Eerdmans Publishing Company.

CHAPTER FOUR

PATRIARCHAL AGE: WILDERNESS WANDERINGS

DISCUSSION QUESTION: Why would God promise Abram land that was occupied by other tribes?

Patriarchal Age

Abram (whose name God changed to Abraham), Isaac, and Jacob (whose name was also changed by God to Israel) were the patriarchs whose lives are recorded in the book of Genesis. They spent most of their lives traveling up and down the Judean Ridge Route which consequently became known as the Way of the Patriarchs in the land of promise. The land of Canaan, as it was then known, was a land inhabited by many tribes. In **Genesis 15:18-21**, there are ten tribes listed as inhabiting the area that the Lord promised Abram. The city-states and tribes from within the Fertile Crescent would frequently wage war on the land of Canaan. A record of one such war is recorded in **Genesis 14**.

Genesis 14

In the first verse of **Genesis 14**, we find Chedorlaomer, the king of Elam; Elam was mentioned in the previous chapter of this book, in historical context, as it relates to the Fertile Crescent. Elam is first mentioned in **Genesis 10:22** as the eldest son of Shem, who was one of the three sons of Noah. In **Genesis 14**, the tribal nation of Elam, under the direction of their king and united with several other tribal nations, made war with Bera, the king of Sodom. There are other city-states or tribal kings mentioned in verse two. In verses three and four, the context of this war is given, verses five through twelve record the war. Abram, upon hearing of the capture of Lot, takes an army and pursues these kings to Hobah which is near Damascus. Some scholars believe that the name of the Kings' Highway was given to the Transjordan Highway as a result of this war.

The city of Sodom was ultimately destroyed by God and only Lot and his two daughters escaped. Through an incestuous relationship with their father, a son was born to each daughter. The people who descended through this incestuous union are the **Moabites** and the **Ammonites**.

Tribes in the Land

In an attempt to bring about God's promise, Abraham fathered Ishmael through Sarah's handmaid Hagar. Ishmael's descendants became known as the **Ishmaelites**. The Ishmaelites became another tribe that inhabited the land of promise when the children of Israel returned from Egypt.

Isaac, who was the son of promise and was born to Abraham in his old age, fathered two sons, Esau and Jacob. The descendants of Esau became known as the **Edomites**, and the descendants of Jacob became known as the **Israelites**. Jacob is the last in the patriarchal line.

Jacob ultimately leads all of the descendants of Abraham down into Egypt. By this time, Abraham and Lot had added to the land of Canaan five more tribes. The **Moabites** and the **Ammonites** had an incestuous heritage through Lot and his daughters. The **Ishmaelites** were the result of Abraham and Sarah's effort to bring about God's promise. The **Midianites** were descendants of Midian born to Abraham through his concubine Keturah. Abraham wanted to protect Isaac's heritage and so he sent them away from Isaac to the east. And finally, we have the tribe of the **Edomites** who were descendants of Esau. Four of these tribes were a result of sin. While Esau's birth was not a result of sin, the enmity between Esau and Jacob was the consequence of Isaac and Rebekah's favoritism. This enmity between the sons of Isaac continued on throughout Israel's history.

[Note: For a detailed study of the conflict between these two brothers, refer to this author's book titled **In His Image**.]

We will now take a closer look at one of the tribes listed in **Genesis 15:19**.

Kenites

The **Kenites** are listed as one of the tribes living in the land the Lord promised to Abraham (**Gen. 15:19**). Their genetic ancestor was Cain (**Gen. 4:16-24**). *Kenite* in Aramaic means "smith" and is believed to refer to the working in bronze that the descendants of Cain are listed as doing.

In **Numbers 24:21-22**, the Kenites are mentioned in Balaam's fourth oracle. You will remember that Balak was in fear of the children of Israel. In **Numbers 22: 1-6**, the children of Israel were camped in Moab, and Balak, who was the king of Moab at this time, was aware of what the Israelites had done to the Amorites. So he and the Midianites agreed to send for Balaam that he might curse the children of Israel. Balaam was in Pethor which was in Mesopotamia, but Balaam was restricted by God from cursing the Israelites much to Balak's frustration. Balaam, instead, blessed Israel and pronounced several oracles on Israel's enemies. In the fourth oracle, he foretold that the **Kenites** would be wasted and carried away captive.

Moses' father-in-law was a Kenite. In **Judges 1:16**, it is recorded that "... *the children of the Kenite, Moses' father-in-law ... left Jericho, the 'city of palm trees', with the children of Judah and lived among them in Arad.*" In **Judges 4:11**, the father-in-law of Moses is again mentioned. "*Heber, the Kenite, of* *the children of Hobab, the father-in-law of Moses."* Hobab is actually the son of Jethro, the father-in-law of Moses.

In **Exodus 2**, the circumstances of Moses' meeting with **Reuel**, also known as **Jethro**, is recorded. Reuel is the name of the clan to which Jethro and Hobab belonged. Jethro, the father-in-law of Moses, is also called **Reuel** in **Exodus 2:18** and **Raguel** in **Numbers 10:29**. These are two forms of his given name. The name *Jethro* was associated with his priestly office. **Exodus 3:1** states, *"the priest of Midian"*, and again in **18:1**, *"Jethro, the priest of Midian."* **Exodus 18:5** records Jethro's relationship to Moses, *". . . Jethro, Moses' father-in-law.*

Hobab was the brother-in-law of Moses, the son of Jethro as explained in **Numbers 10:29**. In **Judges 4:11**, we are introduced to **Heber the Kenite**, the son of Hobab and are told that he moved away from the Kenites. Heber's wife's name was Jael and she is the woman that killed Sisera with a hammer and a tent peg (**Jud. 4:17-22**). In **Judges 5:24**, Jael is called *"blessed among women . . . the wife of Heber the Kenite."*

When Saul was attacking the Amaleks in **1 Samuel 15: 4-6**, he told the Kenites to separate themselves from the Amalekites because they (the Kenites) had shown kindness to the children of Israel when they came out of Egypt. In **1 Samuel 30**, when David led the battle against the Amalekites and returned victorious, the spoils of that battle were shared with those in the cities of the Kenites. They are also mentioned as a people in **1 Samuel 27:10**.

Midianites

You will remember that Midian was the son of Abraham and his concubine Keturah and that Abraham sent them to the east away from Isaac (**Gen. 25:1-6 and 1 Chr. 1:33**). The Midianites were closely associated with the Ishmaelites. They ultimately intermingled in marriage as is seen in the account of Joseph being sold to Midianite traders in **Genesis 37:23-28, 36**. Moses escaped from Egypt to **Midian** and he married into the priestly family of Reuel (**Ex. 2:15-21**). The Midianites joined

Balaam to curse the children of Israel. They harassed and seduced Israel, and were destroyed by Moses (**Num. 22:7, 25:16-18, 31:1-18**). The Midianites lived in the Sinai, Moab, and in the area of Paran [(**1 Ki. 11:18**). They became mixed with the Ishmaelites and eventually became known as the Rechabites.

Rechabites

There is little mentioned of the Rechabites in the Bible. In **1 Chronicles 2:55**, "*And the family of the scribes which dwelt at Jabez . . . These are the Kenites that came of Hemath, the father of the house of Rechab.*" They are listed as scribes, and through genealogy, they are connected to the Kenites that are listed in **Genesis 15: 19** that we have just studied. They trace their heritage back to Hemath who was the father of the house of Rechab. In **2 Kings 10:15-23**, we find mention of Jehonadab, the son of Rechab, but the most interesting mention in scripture of the Rechabites is found in **Jeremiah 35**.

Jeremiah 35 records for us the good example that the Rechabites were. It is a very interesting chapter and I encourage you to read it. But for our purposes, I will summarize it: They refused to drink wine because they had received and followed the instruction from Jonadab to abstain, and God honored them for this. Jeremiah used them as a standard of comparison to others in Israel. In verses **18-19 of Jeremiah 35**, God commended them for their obedience and promised that "*...Rechab shall not want a man to stand before me forever.*" Thus ends the account of the Rechabites in scripture, but there continues to be a historical account of these people.

Historical Accounts 1160 and 1828 AD

Judah Low ben Bezaleel in Nezah Yisrael (Prague 1599) believed the Jews in China to be descended from the Rechabites. And Benjamin of Tudela (1160) found Rechabites in his travels. "Twenty-one day's journey from Babylon, through the desert of Sheba, or Al-Yemen from which Mesopotamia lies directly north, are the abodes of Jews who are called Rechabites." He described them as an independent tribe whose land extends sixteen day's journey among the northern mountains. He said they had fortified cities with the capital city of Tema. Their *nasi* (in Biblical Hebrew means "prince") was Rabbi Hanan. They were marauders allied with nomadic Arabs. They paid tithes for the men learned in the Law, for the poor in Palestine, and for the mourners of Zion and Jerusalem. These mourners wore black, lived in caves and only ate meat on Shabbath.

In 1828, Dr. Wolff, a missionary from England, found Rechabites near Mecca in Arabia. They were observers of the "pure Mosaic Law", they spoke Arabic and some Hebrew, and they were about 60,000 in number. They are descended from Hemath the progenitor of the house of Rechab, otherwise known as Kenites

Wilderness Wanderings

As can be expected, scholars are not agreed on the dates of the wilderness wanderings and consequent entrance into the Promised Land. The following is one possibility for the Wilderness Wanderings based on the year of Jubilee (**Lev. 25:1-9**).

- 1456 BC entered Canaan 1416 BC 1st Jubilee 1367 BC
- Exodus 40 years before **Numbers 32:13**
- Jesus died in 31AD in the middle of the 49th year of the Jubilee cycle which ran from 6AD to 55AD

[Note: Jubilee dates can be calculated starting 6AD and repeatedly subtracting 49 years.]

In **Numbers 33-34**, there is a review of the wilderness wanderings, but for our purposes, we will consider only a few of their stops along the way. In **Deuteronomy 1:19 & 8:15**, the wilderness is referred to as "great and terrible" where there were "fiery serpents and scorpions, and drought". In **32:10**, it is referred to as a "howling wilderness". This is the geographical setting of the children of Israel for forty years. The wilderness wandering was a consequence of their unbelief. They had come to the edge of the Promised Land, and had allowed fear to rob them of their inheritance—they believed a lie. "Giants" were described. They said, *"We are in our own sight as grasshoppers"* (**Num. 13:28, 32-33**). They allowed fear to grip their hearts and they were deceived. Fear will always open you to deception. The consequence was the wandering in the wilderness until that generation died with the exception of Caleb and Joshua.

Kadesh-barnea

Kadesh-barnea, according to some scholars, is located in Transjordan at ancient El Beidha 5 km north of Petra. But most scholars agree that Ein el-Qudeirat is located 27 km east of Wadi Al Arish, which is the Biblical border between Egypt and Israel. Those who argue for the El Beidha location suggest that the Ein el-Qudeirat creates a contradiction in scripture because that placed Kadesh-barnea well within the Promised Land and for that reason it must be rejected.

Israel departed from the Sinai for the Promised Land after spending 11 months and 5 days at Sinai. Since they left on the 14th day of the first month, this means they had been traveling one year, one month and one week since leaving Egypt (57 weeks). They navigated about 20 stops over a period 10.5 and 11 months between Sinai and Kadesh-barnea. After leaving Egypt, they arrived in Kadesh-barnea in the first month of the third year or in exactly 24 months (**Num. 20:1**). There, they celebrated their second Passover at Sinai and then left almost immediately afterward for Kadesh-barnea. After arriving 11 months later, they celebrated their third Passover. They spent 38 continuous years at Kadesh-barnea, and then departed for Jordan in the 40th year. Other scholars believe Kadesh-barnea served as their chief site of encampment. **Psalm 29:8** states, *". . . The Lord shakes the wilderness of Kadesh. . ."* and this is also marked on the Madaba Map, which is an ancient mosaic map found on the floor of a building in Jordan.

It was from Kadesh-barnea that the spies were sent out into Canaan (**Num. 13:1-26**). The first failed attempt to take the land was made from Kadesh-barnea (**Num. 14:40-45**). Then, Moses disobediently struck the rock that brought forth water at this location (**Num. 20:11**). Miriam and Aaron died and were buried nearby (**Num. 20:1, 22-29**). And Moses sent envoys to the King of Edom from Kadesh-barnea asking permission to let the Israelites pass through his terrain (**Num. 20:14**). The Edomite king denied this request. Kadesh-barnea is the common biblical formula delineating the southern border of Israel.

Mt. Hor

Again, scholars disagree on the location of Mt. Hor. One suggested location is in the land of Edom on the east shore of the Dead Sea and the other is by the Mediterranean Sea at the northern border of Israel (**Num. 34:7-8**). The latter is traditionally known as the Nur Mountains, also known as Amanus. In the Bible Atlas, it is suggested to be in Edom based on **Numbers 20:22, 33:37** where Mt Hor is referred to as "... *in the edge of the land of Edom* ..." about a day's journey from Kadesh. Aaron was buried there on Mt. Hor (**Num. 20:28, Dt. 32:50**).

Arad

Arad was an important biblical town in the eastern Negev that dominated the frontier region. It resided at the outset of the highway to Edom and to the harbor of Elath. Arad was an obstacle for the children of Israel on the way to the land of Canaan, "And when the king of Arad, who dwelt in the south, heard tell that Israel came ...he withstood the tribes on their approach from Kadesh-barnea by way of Atharim (**Num. 21:1-3**). But Arad was defeated. As recorded in **Judges 1:16**,. "....*the children of the Kenite, Moses' father-in-law, went up with the people of Judah from the city of palms into the wilderness of Judah, which lies in the Negev near Arad; and they went in and settled with the people.*" There was also a temple found in the ruins of Arad.

Hormah

Hormah was a place of defeat for Israel. Here they were defeated by the Canaanites (**Num. 14:44, and Dt. 1:44**). This defeat is considered to be the explanation of the name by some scholars. Hormah means *devote to destruction.*

Edom

Edom, the name given to Esau, means red, born red, ate red pottage (**Gen. 25:30, and Num. 20:14-21**). Edomites are descendants of Esau. Their territory extended from the Sinai to Kadesh-barnea south to Elath. The boundary between Edom and Moab was Wadi Zered, and their ancient capital was Bozrah, also called Seir, or Mount Seir.

After the Babylonian conquest of Judah, the Edomites settled in Hebron. By the time of Jesus, they were a majority of the population in Western Judea. They were called "*Idumaea*" by the Greeks and Romans. In 125 BC, John Hyrcanus forcibly converted them to Judaism. The book of Obadiah records God's perspective of the Edomites.

Obadiah

The name Obadiah means Servant of God. Little is known about Obadiah. He does his task and disappears, as a good servant should. Obadiah was a contemporary of Jeremiah, the last of the prophets before Israel went into captivity. This is a book that records the story of two brothers, Esau and Jacob. Their story begins in **Genesis 25: 21-28**. Their lives began with a struggle inside their mother's womb and continued most of their lives, resulting in part from the favoritism Rebekah and Isaac showed throughout the lives of these two boys. Eventually, the brothers were reconciled, but the pain they had caused each other was passed on to their children—who carried resentment and bitterness in their hearts—passing it on to future generations.

In **Malachi 1:2**, God states that He has loved Jacob and hated Esau. It was this verse that led me into a study of these brothers. In verse three in the book of Obadiah, we find a clue as to the root cause of this unresolved conflict. Let us look at the continuation of this conflict in terms of the two nations, Israel and Edom.

In **Numbers 20:18-22**, Edom refused to allow Israel to pass through his land using the King's Highway. Moses sent messengers from Kadesh to the king of Edom requesting passage and promising that they would not pass through the Edomites' fields or drink any of their water, but passage was denied them.

In **Exodus 17: 8-16**, we find a record of Israel's war with the Amaleks.

In **1 Chronicles 1:35-36**, Amalek is listed as a descendant of Esau. In **1 Samuel 14:47**, Israel and Edom are at war and in **1 Samuel 15:1-31**, Saul was instructed to REMEMBER what the Amalekites did when they came out of Egypt, and to UTTERLY destroy them. But, we see in verse nine that Saul spared Agag and the best of the herds and flocks.

Second Temple Period

John Hyrcanus forced the Edomites (Idumeans) to convert and gave them full citizenship. In the New Testament, the Edomites are known as Idumeans. The Roman government recognized Herod as king of Judea and the Herodian Jews were in control at the time of Jesus. Under this unrighteous leadership, the Jews used their religion for political gain with the Edomites. This was not the first time in history that religion was used in this way. Jacob's sons used the rite of circumcision for revenge on the men of Shechem. The men of Shechem agreed to circumcision for political gain. Through the policy of expansion and forced conversion, Hyrcanus invited the enemy into Israel. They were given citizenship and through cunning, the enemy gained control until, at the time of the coming of the Messiah, the enemy was on the throne!

REFERENCES

Beitzel, B. J. (1985). *The Moody Atlas of the Bible Lands.* Chicago, IL: Moody Press.

Bromiley, G. W. (Ed.). (1979). *The international standard Bible encyclopedia.* Grand Rapids, MI: Wm. B. Eerdmans Publishing Company.

Morris, H. M. (1995). *The defender's study bible.* Grand Rapids, MI: World Publishing.

Snell, D. C. (1997). *Life in the ancient Near East 3100-332 B.C.E.* New Haven, CT: Yale University Press.

Strong, J. (1947). *Strong's exhaustive concordance of the Bible.* Nashville, TN: Thomas Nelson Publishers.

Tregelles, S. P. (1949). *Hebrew and Chaldee Lexicon.* Grand Rapids, MI: Wm. B. Eerdmans Publishing Company.

Whiston, W. (1999). *The new complete works of Josephus.* Grand Rapids, MI: Kregel Publications.

CHAPTER FIVE

CONQUEST TO JUDGES

DISCUSSION QUESTION: Why was Moses not permitted to enter the Promise Land?

Entering the Land and the Conquest

Following the death of Moses, Joshua and the children of Israel camped at Shittim (which means Acacia Grove) on the plains of Moab, east of the Jordan River and north of the Dead Sea. It was here at Shittim that Israel had *"joined themselves with Baal-peor"*. They played the harlot through uniting with the daughters of Moab (Num. 25:1-5).

- Moses took a census of Israel here at Shittim. Numbers 26 records this census.
- Revenge was taken on the Midianites and Balaam was slain here in Shittim. In Micah 6:3-5, the Lord reminds the children of Israel of the ordeal with Balaak and Balaam and reminds them that He had demonstrated His righteousness from "Acacia Grove (Shittim) to Gilgal" (**Num. 31:1-20**).
- Here, the tribes of Rueben and Gad took portions of Transjordan as their inheritance.

The children of Israel camped at Shittim for three days—three days of facing the impossible—the raging Jordan River. They knew that they would need a miracle to cross the river.

They were, in fact, facing the impossible from a place of previous failure, a place where they had committed idolatry. Do you think the average person among them was fearful? As they faced their fear for these three days, do you think they were remembering God's mercy and forgiveness?

Joshua sent two spies to spy out the land. As is well known, they came to Jericho and were protected by Rahab the harlot. Rahab told the spies that everyone in Jericho had heard all that the Lord their God had done for them since they left Egypt and that everyone was in fear because of them (**Josh. 2:9-11**). It must have been encouraging for the spies to see how the Lord had gone before them and even more so for Joshua when they reported back to him.

Crossing the Jordan

Prior to crossing the Jordan River, the people were given detailed instructions. They were to wait until they saw the priests and the Levites carrying the Ark of the Covenant before they moved. The Ark of the Covenant was the representation of God with them. They were further instructed to keep a distance between them and the Ark and not to come near it. In **Joshua 3:5**, they are instructed to "*. . . sanctify yourselves for tomorrow the Lord will do wonders among you.*"

At this time, the Jordan River was overflowing its banks, but when the priests stepped into the river, the waters of the Jordan were blocked at Adam and Zarethan, 16 miles north of Jericho. The priests stood firm with the Ark on dry ground in the midst of the river. There was a dry bed for 20 miles between Adam and the Dead Sea. This was not a narrow passageway (**Josh. 3:15-17**). The priests were the first to enter the river and the last to leave.

Gilgal

When they came out of the Jordan, they camped at Gilgal which was located on the east border of Jericho. There were about 40,000 men prepared for war among them (**Josh. 4:13**). From the towers of the walls of Jericho, Gilgal was easily in view. The children of Israel were now in enemy territory and in plain sight of their enemies, and they were required to become circumcised! In essence, they were told to make themselves vulnerable in enemy territory (**Josh. 5:2-8**). But **in verse one of chapter five**, their enemies are described as in fear of them and without the spirit to fight as a result of the Lord drying up the waters of the Jordan.

Do you remember the account of Jacob's sons slaughtering all the men of Shechem who had been circumcised and were unable to defend themselves? In **Genesis 34:25**, it states that the sons of Jacob attacked the men of Shechem on the third day when they were sore and unable to fight. Circumcision, at Gilgal, would have rendered the 40,000 men of war vulnerable. Today, with modern surgical procedures it takes an adult male a week to recover from this procedure.

There on the plains of Jericho, on the fourteenth day of the month, the children of Israel kept the Passover. So, since crossing the Jordan into enemy territory, they took the time to set up a memorial to their crossing, the adult males were circumcised, and they celebrated the Passover. At least a week, but most probably more, had passed since their crossing the Jordan, and they seemed to be doing nothing to prepare for battle. Yet, in reality, they were doing *spiritual battle*. They were remembering the greatness of the God who is was leading them, and renewing their commitment to Him.

Finally, they began their conquest of the land by marching around Jericho. JERICHO is known as the *back door* to the Promised Land (the front door, Gezer, is on the coast). It was known as this because it was located strategically guarding three routes that lead to the Way of the Patriarchs (Judean Ridge Route) then on to the Coastal Highway through the Benjamin Plateau. Coming from the Wilderness Wanderings, there was no better place, no location more strategically beneficial for the taking of the land than Jericho. How would the children of Israel know that? They had never been in the land.

They would not have known this, BUT the Lord knew and He was guiding them.

Ai

The strategy for taking Ai was an ambush. This involved tactical planning by Joshua. He maneuvered his forces to take the maximum advantage of the terrain. The Israelites' "base camp" was situated north of Bethel and Ai beyond the valley which contained seasonal wadis. The problem facing Joshua was how to attack this strong enemy force without exposing his flank and rear, and without losing the element of surprise. He solved this difficulty by appearing to repeat the earlier tactical mistake, but in actuality, moving secretly a large ambush of 30,000 men into position west some 36 hours before the attack began. The smaller ambush, of about 5,000 men, was assigned their positions on the eve of the battle (Josh. 8:14).

When all the preparations were complete, Joshua camped in the valley north of Ai. When the reserve troops of Bethel hurriedly pursued the supposing fleeing Israelites (Josh. 8:15), the 30,000 men rose up and attacked the enemy in the rear while the smaller force sacked and burned Bethel. Ai opened the way up the ridge that formed the backbone of the land, and Joshua was able to lead them unopposed to Mt. Ebal and Mt. Gerizim, which we previously discussed in our study of Shechem.

Gibeonites (Joshua 9)

Joshua 9:1-2 is an introduction, a background, for the account that will be told in the rest of this chapter. The context is the alliance of these kings. Notice the description of where the kings were located: this side of the Jordan, in the hills, the valleys, and the coasts. In other words, these kings were representative of the tribes throughout the land.

The Hivites, also known throughout scripture as the Horites, the Hurrians, and the Gibeonites (who were said to be their descendants, being an off-shoot of the Amorites) became concerned with the threat of the children of Israel. They must have considered resistance to be futile and came up with a plan in the hope of survival. Beeroth was located near to Ai and might be the next place of attack. The inhabitants of Beeroth were Hivites and their capital city was Gibeon.

They came up with a plan: if you can't beat them, join them. But somehow the Hivites knew that the children of Israel were not going to make peace treaties with the inhabitants of Canaan, therefore, they presented themselves as inhabitants of a distant land.

Of interest to me is how the Gibeonites knew that the children of Israel would not make a peace treaty with them? Why go through this elaborate charade when you could just offer a peace treaty? The Gibeonites, according to the clear instructions of the Lord, were the enemy. Yet, here we have the enemy aware of the directives that the children of Israel had received, and with that awareness, developed a strategy that would lead them into compromise.

Do you know that the enemy strategizes over you? In the book of Job 1:8, when Satan is before the Lord, he is asked, "... have you considered my servant Job?" The word translated *"considered"* is actually two Hebrew words, one of which means *"considered."* But putting these two words together, as it is in the Hebrew, it would be more correctly translated *"strategized"*. Your enemy knows where you are vulnerable.

The children of Israel looked at the circumstances and believed a lie. Have you ever done that? Have you ever looked at your circumstances instead of to the Lord and drew a conclusion based on those circumstances? They made peace with their enemy, not just Joshua, but the princes as well. It was a unanimous decision.

Because they made a league with them, the children of Israel were obligated to defend them if the Gibeonites came under attack—which happened almost immediately after the agreement was made. Although dismayed by their deception, Israel honored their agreement and the Gibeonites became hewers of wood and drawers of water for the congregation and for the altar of the Lord. The Gibeonites are listed in Nehemiah along with the captives returning from captivity. In **Nehemiah 3:7**, a Gibeonite is listed among those rebuilding the wall of Jerusalem. In **Nehemiah 7:25**, they are listed with the Israelite families who returned to Jerusalem from exile: The children of Gibeon, ninety and five.

Biblical Amorites

The term Amorites is used in the Bible to refer to certain highland mountaineers who inhabited the land of Canaan. They are described in **Genesis 10:16** as descendants of Canaan, son of Ham. They are described as a powerful people of great stature "like the height of the cedars who occupied the land east and west of the Jordan" (**Amos 2:9**). This reference to their height has led some scholars to refer to the Amorites as "giants". The Amorite king Og, was the last of the remnant of the Rephaim (**Dt. 3:11**). The terms Amorite and Canaanite seem to be interchangeable, with Canaanite being more general and Amorite a more specific component among the Canaanites who occupied the land.

The Biblical Amorites seem to have originally occupied the region stretching from the heights west of the Dead Sea to Hebron (**Dt. 3:8, 4:46-48**), embracing all of Gilead and all of Bashan (**Dt. 3:10**) with the Jordan Valley on the east of the river being the land of the "two kings of the Amorites", Sihon and Og (**Dt. 31:4, and Josh. 2:10, 9:10**). Both Sihon and Og were independent kings. These Amorites seem to have been linked to the Jerusalem region, and the Jebusites may have been a subgroup of them. The southern slopes of the mountains of Judea are called the "mount of the Amorites" (**Dt. 1:7, 19, 20**).

Joshua Ten

Here we pick up the account of the Amorites and the battle in defense of Gibeon. The effect of the political situation was immediate. The Hivites-Gibeonites formed a formidable state. Their cities were well placed on the southern highland. Gibeon, the capital, was one of the most important fortresses of the district which was about five miles northwest of Jerusalem at the eastern end of the Valley of Aijalon.

The king of Jerusalem was in fear of the advancing army of invaders. When it was just Jericho and Ai that had been defeated there was no great danger, they were just other tribes, other city-states that now had a different administration. But, when the news came that the Gibeonites had allied with the foreigners, this was reason for concern.

The Amorites recognized at once that, in view of this important defection, it was imperative for them to crush the Gibeonites before the Israelites could unite with them.

The king of Jerusalem sent an urgent message to four other kings: Hebron, Jarmuth, Lachish, and Eglon. The Gibeonites send an urgent message to Joshua at Gilgal, his base camp. I can imagine that Joshua was not happy upon receiving this call for help from those by whom he had been deceived. But he obviously put the matter before the Lord, because the Lord assured Joshua of complete victory.

We are not told by which route Joshua and his men marched, but it is significant that the Amorites fled by the way of Beth-horon, not towards their own cities. Joshua had succeeded in cutting off their retreat to Jerusalem. The greater part of the Amorite army escaped. The armies of the five kings were on the run when the Lord cast down great stones from heaven.

God intervened in this key battle demonstrating to the sun-worshipping, moon-worshipping, nature-worshipping Canaanites, that He controlled the forces of nature. These "great stones" from heaven were possibly from a volcanic eruption. The "hailstones" implies a unique atmospheric upheaval, probably caused by the swift deceleration of the earth's rotation. Joshua asked the Lord to stop the rotation of the earth: Sun, stand thou still upon Gibeon; and thou Moon, in the valley of Aijalon. (Josh. 10:12)

A gradual deceleration of the earth to a stop, then the gradual acceleration again to its normal speed would generate profound atmospheric disturbances since the normal circulation of the atmosphere is tied in closely with the earth's rotation. It might even have caused volcanic activity. The earth's interior magma circulation would also be influenced to some degree by its rotation. Stopping a planetary rotation and simultaneously stopping a lunar revolution is the sole explanation satisfying all the descriptions of this event.

The Lord God, Creator of the universe, established an orderly universe. In this case, He chose to respond to Joshua's prayer and disrupt that order. This was an incredible miracle, God does work miraculously and when He does so, He makes the decision from eternity.

There are certain realities that we can depend upon, such as the sun rising and setting, the seasons, if we plant seeds for flowers we will not harvest garlic. There is an order that we can depend upon. Order is the rule we can be sure of. If miracles were the rule, we would live in a chaotic universe. If every time one of us prayed for a miracle and it was answered, then miracles would be the rule, and chaos would be our reality. God does act miraculously, but He does so from an eternal perspective.

Joshua continued to lead in the conquest and finally, in the distribution of the land.

<u>Time of the Judges</u>

Jewish historians claim that Judges "ruled" only at extraordinary times, such as making war on a common enemy. In times of peace, they served a judicial function. Most judges were only of local importance. The "Great Judges" influence was confined to one of a few tribes. Neither the life nor the law was fully regulated.

- Deborah (Jud. 4:1-5:31)
- Jephthah (Jud. 11)

The primary ministry of Old Testament Prophets was to give divine interpretation to historical events. The earliest example is that of an unnamed prophet (Jud. 6:7-10).

Local Enemies

The dominant powers were not involved in the area during the time of the judges. The wars Israel fought were with local tribes from:
- Mesopotamia
- Moab
- Canaan
- Midian
- Ammon
- Philistia

The book of Ruth was written during the time of the judges. In **Ruth 1:1**, we are told that there was a famine in the land. A famine in Israel was a result of God's judgment. To escape the famine (i.e. God's judgment), Naomi follows her husband to Moab.

Moabites

In **Genesis 19: 37**, Moab is listed as the son of Lot's eldest daughter, born of an incestuous relationship between Lot and his daughter. The Moabites are the descendants of Moab. The country of Moab was bordered by the Dead Sea, the Jordan River, the country of Ammon (descendants of Lot through the younger daughter) and the Arabian Desert.

There is very little archeological evidence of the existence of the Moabites prior to the children of Israel's return from Egypt. Their existence before the return is known archaeologically from a colossal statue erected in Luxor by Pharaoh Ramesses II which lists Mu'ab among the nations conquered during a campaign.

The Moabites enjoyed the protection of Egypt because the country of Moab was strategically located and gave the Egyptians control of the Sinai. The King's Highway (Transjordan Highway) ran through Moab and Egypt. When trading with Damascus, they used this international highway to move their goods.

In **Deuteronomy 23:3-5** it reads, An Ammonite or Moabite shall not enter into the congregation of the Lord, even to their tenth generation... *Because they met you not with bread and water... when you came out of Egypt; and because they hired against you Balaam, the son of Beor of Pethor of Mesopotamia, to curse you...*

The enmity between Israel and Moab existed from the time of Israel's wanderings in the wilderness. During the reign of Rehoboam, Moab was absorbed into the northern kingdom's realm as a vassal state. This continued until the death of Ahab when the Moabites refused to pay tribute and went to war against Israel. During the reign of Jehoram under king Mesha, the Moabites attacked again but were defeated near En-Gedi. Once again, in the year of Elisha's death, they invaded Israel, and later, aided Nebuchadnezzar in his campaign against Jehoiakim.

During the Persian period, Moab disappeared from the historical record. Tribes from northern Arabia, most notably the Nabateans, overran the territory of Moab. By the time of Nehemiah, the Arabs were mentioned as allies with the Ammonites, but there was no mention of Moab.

Ruth

Ruth was a Moabite, and according to **Deuteronomy 23:2-3**, "*...no bastard... or Moabite shall enter into the congregation of the Lord... to the tenth generation...*"

In the genealogy of Jesus found in **Matthew 1:1-16**, both Pharez (v. 3) and Obed (v. 5) are listed. Pharez was the illegitimate son of Judah and Tamar; Obed was the son of Boaz and Ruth, a Moabite. Obed became the father of Jesse and Jesse, the father of David, the line through which the Messiah Jesus came. David was free from the exclusion because the prohibition was for a Moabite. Ruth was a Moabitess. This reference is according to rabbinical sources.

It is interesting to me that Boaz, who was an older man with wealth, was not married. It was, and still is in Israel, important for a man to marry and have children. Yet, Boaz had not married. Through the genealogy of Jesus, we learn that the mother of Boaz was Rachab, the harlot from Jericho. Is it possible that there was a stigma attached to Boaz because of this lineage? Is it possible that no father would agree to give his daughter to the son of a prostitute because of the shame it would bring on the family name?

Boaz was certainly sensitive to Ruth's situation as a Moabite, a foreigner, and made arrangements to provide for and protect her. Perhaps this was because he was remembering the hardship his mother endured as a foreigner in Israel. The book of Ruth—which records the story of Ruth, the Moabite and Boaz, the son of a prostitute—is a beautiful love story. It is a demonstration of the heart of Father God, who engineered this love story, and who was not ashamed to have the name of Rachab listed in the genealogy of His family line.

༄

REFERENCES

Beitzel, B. J. (1985). *The Moody Atlas of the Bible Lands.* Chicago, IL: Moody Press.

Bromiley, G. W (Ed.). (1979). *The international standard Bible encyclopedia.* Grand Rapids, MI: Wm. B. Eerdmans Publishing Company.

Morris, H. M. (1995). *The defender's study bible.* Grand Rapids. MI: World Publishing.

Snell, D. C. (1997). *Life in the Ancient Near East 3100-332 B.C.E.* New Haven, CT: Yale University Press.

Strong, J. (1947). *Strong's Exhaustive Concordance of the Bible.* Nashville, TN: Thomas Nelson Publishers.

Tregelles, S. P. (1949). *Hebrew and Chaldee Lexicon.* Grand Rapids, MI: Wm. B. Eerdmans Publishing Company.

Whiston, W. (1999). *The new complete works of Josephus.* Grand Rapids, MI: Kregel Publications.

CHAPTER SIX

PRIESTS AND LEVITES SAMUEL-SOLOMON

DISCUSSION QUESTION: What is the role of Prophecy?

Priests

Priests were male descendants of Aaron the High Priest, brother of Moses of the tribe of Levi, who were consecrated to serve in the priesthood of the Tabernacle, and later in the Temple. Their tasks included the offering of sacrifices, the burning of incense, and the arranging of the showbread. They did not receive an allotment of their own since they earned their livelihood from priestly gifts, such as parts of the sacrifices, firstborn flocks and cattle, first fruits, and tithes. Their status also imposed upon them prohibitions and restrictions, such as being forbidden to come in contact with a dead person, or to marry a divorced woman.

At the head of the priestly hierarchy stood the High Priest, whose special duties included the Temple service on the Day of Atonement. Essentially, the priest's duties were confined to matters of worship. However, in the period of the Judges and the First Temple, he was assigned additional responsibilities. He conveyed the word of God to the nation, was approached regarding inquiries to God, was a teacher instructing the nation in Torah, rendered judgment on questions of ritual impurity, and served in legal matters. In the days of the Second Temple, the High Priests became political leaders.

Decoding the Priesthood

New genetic research shows the vast majority of "kohaim" (the Jewish priestly class) to be descended from a single ancestor—scientific confirmation of an oral tradition passed down through 3,000 years.

Since the late 90s, there has been a worldwide project to study the ancient lineage of the Jewish priesthood. The cells taken through mouth swabs of Jews across the world have revealed that at least 70 percent of the *kohaim* have a common set of markers on their Y chromosome. Every male receives this chromosome *unchanged* from his father. Researchers have concluded that the Jewish priesthood has a genetic basis that points to a single ancestor, and that ancestor would be Aaron. As is well known, you can convert to Judaism, but you cannot convert into the priesthood. This gene trail may lead all the way back to Jacob (Israel)!

Levites

The Levites are members of the Levite tribe which is not included in the order of the priests. Like the priests, they were chosen by Moses to serve in the Tabernacle as a reward for their loyalty to him regarding the golden calf. During the wanderings in the wilderness, they were charged with carrying the Tabernacle and its holy vessels, and helping the priests. They did not receive territories of their own, but were allotted 48 cities and subsisted from the tithes they received from the people.

When the First Tabernacle was built, the Levites were divided into 24 watches of the priests. Among the Levites, judges, officials, public teachers, and the Torah scribes, were appointed. During the Second Temple period, their duties were confined to singers, musicians, gatekeepers, and public servants. The Levites were ranked second to the priests in the social hierarchy and above the rank of *Israel*. *Israel* refers to a person who is a Jew but is neither a priest nor a Levite.

"Simon and Levi are brethren; instruments of cruelty are in their habitations . . . Cursed be their anger . . . I will divide them in Jacob, and scatter them in Israel" (**Gen. 49:5-7**). The

cruelty ascribed to Levi in this verse refers to the time he and his brother Simon took vengeance on the men of Shechem for the defilement of their sister Dinah. It is foretold, as a curse, that they would be scattered throughout Israel. This was fulfilled, but the Lord had turned it around into a blessing when the land was divided, and the Levites were given cities among each of the tribes as spiritual leaders.

- Exodus 6:16: They were divided into three families; Gershom, Kohath, and Amram.
- Exodus 28:1: Aaron was the great-grandson of Levi, who was chosen for the priesthood.
- Deuteronomy 10:8-9: They were chosen for ministry to receive no inheritance (i.e. no land allotment). There were Levitical cities within each tribe's allotment (Josh. 21).
- Numbers 1:47-54: The Levites were not numbered. "... behold, I have taken the Levites from among the children of Israel instead of all the firstborn that open the matrix among the children of Israel: therefore the Levites shall be mine..."
- Numbers 3: 6-14: Substituted for Israel's firstborn.
- Numbers 8:5-26: Describes the dedication of the Levites unto the Lord.
- Numbers 16:1-40: Korah, who was a son of Levi Izhar, not through Aaron, rebelled against Moses and Aaron. Korah and those with him were buried alive.
- Numbers 17:1-13, 18:1-2: Aaron's position as High Priest is confirmed through the blossoming of his rod. In chapter eighteen verses one and two, "... *The Lord said unto Aaron, you and your sons, and your father's house ... shall bear the iniquity of the sanctuary: you and your sons will bear the iniquity of the priesthood ... also the tribe of Levi may be joined with you, and minister unto you: but you and your sons shall minister before the tabernacle of witness.*"

The Lord Himself was to be Aaron's portion. "*... you shall have no inheritance in the land . . . I am your part and inheritance. I have given the children of Levi the tenth in Israel for an inheritance*". The Lord provided cities for the Levite's, and after the conquest of the land, Joshua assigned them those cities (Num. 35:2-8, Jos. 14:3-4).

Samuel

Samuel was a judge, a priest and also a prophet (1 Sam. 7:9, 13:11-14). In 1 Samuel 19:20 it reads, "And Saul sent messengers to take David: and when they saw the company of the prophets prophesying and Samuel standing as appointed over them, the Spirit of God was upon the messengers of Saul, and they also prophesied." Samuel was obviously the leader of this company of prophets. It is probable that Samuel was the founder of the "school of the prophets" referred to in 2 Kings 2:25, "*From Bethel Elisha passed on to Mt. Carmel, the home of the school of the prophets...*"

Prophets

In **Genesis 20:7**, Abraham is called a prophet by God when in a dream Abimelech is warned that Sarah is Abraham's wife: "*... he is a prophet, and he will pray for you...*" Aaron is mentioned as a prophet in **Exodus 7:1**: "*... and Aaron, thy brother, shall be thy prophet.*" Exodus 15:20 says, "*And Miriam the prophetess, the sister of Aaron, took a timbrel in her hand; and all the women went out after her...*"

From these verses, we see that prophets would intercede in prayer, would speak for God to man, and would lead in worship. There were prophetesses as well as prophets. When the children of Israel entered the land, the Lord continued to raise up prophets. 1 Samuel 2:27-36, "*And there came a man of God to Eli, and said unto him, Thus saith the Lord...*" These verses record for us the message of an unknown prophet to Eli the priest. The Old Testament records many of the messages of the prophets in books titled after their names.

But consider this. What was the role of prophets and their prophecies? Prophets clearly demonstrated that God existed outside of time, since many messages foretold future events. Prophetic messages also brought warnings of consequences from God to His people when they were walking in disobedience. Perhaps the best known prophecy is found in **Isaiah 53** which foretells the suffering and death of Jesus.

The question to you is this: Does a prophetic message carry with it God's approval? For example, consider the prophecy in Isaiah concerning the crucifixion of Jesus. If you were alive at that time, would you have participated in His crucifixion because it had been prophesied? I'd like you to think about this because we will be looking at this issue again when we discuss Modern Israel. For now, let us return to Samuel.

During this period in the history of Israel, the enemy they were in conflict with was the Philistines, a local tribe who were within the land and whom they were instructed to conqueror and destroy. But after receiving great victories from the Lord in the conquest of the land, the people tired of war and were willing to settle for the land they had already taken. Thus, the Philistines remained, and became an enemy that consistently reared its ugly head.

During one of these battles, Eli's sons took the Ark of the Covenant into battle against the Philistines as a good luck charm. The Ark was at Shiloh in the Tabernacle.

Shiloh

The significance of Shiloh is that the Tabernacle and the Ark of the Covenant dwelt there. Within the Ark of the Covenant were the two stone tablets on which the Ten Commandments were written, Aaron's rod that budded, and the golden pot of manna (**Heb. 9:4-5**). The mercy seat covered the Law. And it was above the Mercy seat that God would meet with the

High Priest once a year on the Day of Atonement when he brought in the sacrificial blood.

After the conquest, Joshua apportioned the land from Shiloh for the home of the tabernacle. Shiloh is located between Shechem and Bethel, 17 kilometers south of Shechem in Samaria. Shiloh is on the ridge of the mountains in the fertile area of Ephraim, and on the Way of the Patriarchs (Judean Ridge Route). During the Canaanite period it was an ancient city of worship. Archeologists have uncovered their ritual vessels as well as a statue of a bull that was used in cult worship on this site.

Historically, conquering-armies-would build a temple to their gods on the site where those who were defeated had worshipped. Perhaps this is why Israel chose Shiloh for the dwelling place of the *Tabernacle* (Tent of Meeting). It remained there for 369 years according to the Talmud.

Philistines Capture the Ark

The children of Israel lost this battle and the Ark of the Covenant was captured by the Philistines. Several interesting things happened to the Philistines and their god Dagon as a result. The Philistines were plagued with tumors, and or possibly the bubonic plague. Their handmade god was brought on his face before the true and living God. As a result, the Philistines wanted to get rid of the tabernacle, and it was sent to Israel at Beth-Shemesh.

Men at Beth-Shemesh

In **1 Samuel 6: 19** it says, *"And He smote the men of Beth-Shemesh, because they looked into the ark of the Lord, even He smote of the people fifty thousand and threescore and ten and ten men..."* The men of Beth-Shemesh lifted the Mercy Seat and looked upon the Law. They were in the Presence of the Lord without the covering of His mercy. The ark was then moved to Kirjath-jearim where it remained for twenty years.

Under Samuel's leadership, the children of Israel repented and put away Baalim and Ashtaroth and *"served the Lord only"* (**1 Sam. 7:4**). The Lord then gave them victory over the Philistines. 1 Samuel 7:13-14 records for us that the Philistines were subdued and the cities they had taken were returned to Israel and that there was peace between Israel and the Amorites.

There are complicated formulas that offer various dates for the reigns of Saul and David. For the purpose of this study, I am simply choosing from the various dates suggested by scholars who are more qualified than I to make such estimates.

Saul 1052—1010 BC

Acts 13:20-21 says, *"And after that He gave unto them judges for the space of four hundred and fifty years; until Samuel, the prophet. And afterward they desired a king; and He gave unto them Saul. . .*

Saul began his reign in about 1025 BC and reigned for forty years according to this scripture in Acts. During the first twenty years of his reign, Samuel was still alive. The enemies that Saul battled with were local. The great empires of Mesopotamia were on the rise, but not yet aggressive in the Levant. In **1 Samuel 1:6-10**, it is recorded that an Amalekite killed Saul—at Saul's request. It is interesting to note that the Amalekites were still in existence at the end of Saul's reign, since he had been instructed to utterly destroy them.

David - 1010—970 BC

David was anointed king by Samuel but did not function in that role until approximately fifteen years later. Most of those years were spent running and hiding from Saul. Following Saul's death, David obeyed the Lord's leading and moved to Hebron where he was crowned king of Judah. Abner, the captain of Saul's army, anointed Ish-bosheth king of Israel, who reigned for two years. Led by Abner, the armies of Ish-bosheth warred with the army of David. This is the first time the kingdom was divided. After many years, a truce was drawn between David and Abner, and David began his reign over all of Israel.

With the nation united, David fought the Jebusites in Jerusalem. After this victory, he moved from Hebron (he had dwelled in Hebron for seven and a half years). After defeating the Philistines, David moved the Ark of the Covenant to Jerusalem, known also as the City of David, and as Zion.

During David's reign, he fought against the Philistines, Moabites, the king of Zobah all the way to the border of the Euphrates, the Syrians, and Ammonites. Again, you will note these are local tribes and kingdoms. The civil wars in Israel, and the battles within the family of David had a more devastating effect on the kingdom than did its wars with these tribes.

Nathan was a prophet during David's reign.

Solomon 970—930 BC

During Solomon's reign, he built and dedicated the Temple in Jerusalem, and moved the Ark of the Covenant there. It remained until, according to legend, it was taken to Ethiopia by one of Solomon's sons through the Queen of Sheba. Ethiopian Jews, known as Falasha Jews, declare that their heritage traces back to a union between King Solomon and the Queen of Sheba.

Solomon married seven hundred wives who were representative of political alliances. These wives led him into *idolatry*. Solomon built a high place for Chemosh and for Molech on the Mt. of Olives, one of seven hills surrounding Jerusalem. The worship of these gods of Moab and Ammon by Solomon resulted in the kingdom of Israel being permanently divided. The word of the Lord to Solomon concerning the division of the kingdom was confirmed through Ahijah the prophet.

Solomon trusted in the political alliances that he had made through marriage to maintain peace. For the most part, his reign was a peaceful one, but he was not without adversaries. Among his adversaries were Hadad the Edomite (who was taken to Egypt when Joab, the captain of David's army, was attempting to kill every male in Edom), Rezon, the son of Eliadah (who fled from Zobah and went to Damascus when David slew Zobah who reigned over Syria), and Jeroboam, an Ephrathite from Zereda (whom Solomon sought to kill after the prophet Ahijah foretold the division of the kingdom). Rehoboam sought refuge in Egypt. Jeroboam was the instrument used to rend the kingdom of Israel.

Syria and Egypt

It is interesting to note here that Solomon's enemies sought refuge in countries that would later become involved both politically and militarily in the northern kingdom of Israel and in Judah. At this time, the great empires of Mesopotamia were beginning to extend their borders, and they were hungry for conquests in the Levant. Israel would never again know the peace they enjoyed during Solomon's reign.

CR

REFERENCES

Bromiley, G. W. (Ed.) (1979). *The international standard Bible encyclopedia.* Grand Rapids, MI: Wm. B. Eerdmans Publishing Company.

Harrison, R.K. (Ed.). (1988). *The new Unger's Bible dictionary.* Chicago, IL: Moody Press.

Hirshberg, P. (Report May 20, 1999). *Decoding the priesthood.* Jerusalem, IL: The Jerusalem Report.

Richman, C. (1997). *A house of prayer for all nations: The holy temple of Jerusalem.* Jerusalem, IL: The Temple Institute, Carta, Jerusalem.

Whiston, Wm. (1999). *The new complete works of Josephus.* Grand Rapids, MI: Kregel Publications.

CHAPTER SEVEN

DIVIDED KINGDOM-CAPTIVITY

DISCUSSION QUESTION: What is the difference between a King and a Judge?

[Note to Instructor: You may prefer to divide this chapter into several sessions as it covers so much history. In addition to setting Israel in context of Mesopotamia's political developments, it is also intended to show how oblivious God's chosen people were to the coming threat of Assyria and Babylon. The divided kingdom was so preoccupied with their civil wars and local threats that they were blind to the bigger picture, and to the coming judgment of the Lord. When that judgment came, and they were under attack, instead of turning away from the idol worship that placed them in this position and calling on the Lord for deliverance, they called on their enemies for help.

The northern kingdom of Israel turned to her enemy Syria to fight against her brother Judah, the southern kingdom. Judah called on Assyria to deliver them, and paid tribute to the Assyrians for their deliverance. This pattern of internal strife, and turning to the enemy for deliverance is a pattern that continued throughout their history. This chapter will not cover every political leader during that period, only those that were either relevant or will help to convey the development of Assyria and then Babylon. The chapter will end with the fall of the northern kingdom and with Judah going into Babylonian captivity. Because it covers hundreds of years, you may want to slow it down a bit and divide the chapter. It would be beneficial to create a detailed Timeline using the overhead projector or whiteboard to help the student assimilate the chronology of this history.]

Assyria-Babylon-Egypt

Assyria emerged as a military power during the end of Solomon's reign (935—913 BC). By 884 to 860 BC, the concept of dominance and methods of warfare were developed by Ashurnasirpal II. Assyria had a standing army and was famous for their ruthlessness. The plan behind their methods was to consolidate the states within the empire and to gain control of the trade routes. The international trade routes were the Via Maris (Coastal Highway), and the King's Highway (Transjordan Highway). The passes connecting these international highways ran through Israel and therefore placed her in the direct line of fire.

Ashur-dan II: 935—912 BC

Ashur-dan II expanded the territory of the Assyrians to the foothills of Arbel: Mt. Arbel is in the Lower Galilee near Tiberius. Ashur-dan II gave ploughs to all throughout the land resulting in a record grain harvest, which no doubt strengthened the Assyrians. This was a brilliant strategy for keeping peace at home and the country united.

Mt. Arbel

Mt. Arbel is located in the lower Galilee on the northwest side of the Sea of Galilee. From the heights of Arbel, one can see Mt. Hermon and the Sea of Galilee. There are many caves in the mountain that have been used for shelter throughout history. The Jews hid there from Herod the Great. He dropped his soldiers down in baskets to the level of the caves to attack them. Some believe the reference in **Isaiah 9:2** to the *"shadow of death"* refers to the shadow that the Arbel casts. The only mention in scripture of Mt. Arbel is in **Hosea 10:14**, *"Therefore shall a tumult arise among your people, and all your fortresses shall be spoiled, as Shalman spoiled Beth-Arbel in the day of battle....."* This is a reference to the Assyrians. [Note: it is spelled "Shalman" in the KJV and is in Hosea]

Divided Kingdom: 909—886 BC

Israel, as a nation, was weakened by their disunity. Jerusalem remained the capital of Judah, the southern kingdom. Shechem became the capital of Israel, the northern kingdom. These two kingdoms often joined with their historic enemies to war against each other. In **1 Kings 15:16**, it is recorded that there was war between Asa, the king of Judah, and Baasha, the king of Israel, all their days.

In 1Kings 15:16-20, King Asa took all the valuable vessels from the temple and sent them to Ben-hadad in payment for aligning with Judah against King Baasha of Israel. Ben-hadad broke the league he had with Baasha and joined Asa. Ben-hadad took the northern cities and the land of Naphtali as his booty of war.

After the death of Zimri, who was king of Israel for seven days, there was a division in the northern kingdom. Half the people wanted to follow Tibni, half followed Omri. Those who followed Omri prevailed and he became King of Israel. Omri changed the capital of the northern kingdom to Samaria which was situated strategically on a hill. He reigned for twelve years and was succeeded by his son Ahab (**1 Ki. 16:21-28**).

Meanwhile, Assyria was a threat rising on the horizon. Under Tukulti-Ninurta II from 890—884 BC, they expanded their territories in the north, west of Mesopotamia and opened the way to the Anatolia. Among the peoples inhabiting these new territories were the Armenians.

Armenia

The Armenians date back to an inscription in the territories conquered by Naram-Sin in 2300 BC. It was then an Akkadian colony (the confederate kingdom of Nairi) between 1500 BC and 1200 BC. At the time of Jonah's preaching (760 BC), they were a part of the Assyrian Empire. I mention this here because of the relevance this will hold later in our studies of the early church.

The Armenians allied with the Hittites and defeated the Assyrians in 714 BC; then they aligned with the Medes in 612 BC. During the time of Tigranes the Great, the Armenia state was the strongest state east of the Roman Empire.

Israel-Assyria

During Omri's reign in Israel, Ashur-Nasir pal II (883—859 BC) was consolidating territories and the new Assyrian Empire was established. This empire became known for the atrocities committed on captives and for transplanting surviving captives to other lands throughout their empire.

Ahab became king of Israel (874—853 BC). Asa was king of Judah as recorded in 1Kings 16: 29-30; this was during the reign of Shalmaneser III of Assyria. Ahab and his wife Jezebel are infamous for their idol worship and their wickedness. The Prophet Elijah's prophecies brought great distress to Ahab, but did not bring him to repentance.

Ben-hadad of Syria declared war on Israel and an unnamed prophet foretold Ahab's victory in 1 Kings 20:13-15, and in **verse 34**, Ahab makes a covenant with the defeated Ben-hadad. The remainder of the chapter is the prophecy against Ahab by another unknown prophet, because of the covenant he had made with Ben-hadad.

So, although the Assyrian Empire was on the move, the battles in Israel and Judah were still with local rivals. In **1 Kings 22:29-40**, Ahab talked Jehoshaphat, king of Judah, into joining him in battle to take Ramoth-Gilead from the Syrians. Ahab was killed in this battle.

Unknown prophets mentioned during Ahab's time: Elijah and Elisha.

This brings us now in Assyrian history to the time of Shalmaneser III (859—824 BC). This is the Shalman mentioned in **Hosea 10:14**. Shalmaneser III waged a constant series of campaigns to the east. The first time Assyria came into direct conflict with Israel was in 842 BC (Israel paid tribute). However, local conflicts continued with Syria, Moab, and Edom.

During this time, the kingdom of Judah was under the influence of the house of Ahab, because Jehoshaphat—in an effort to align the northern and southern kingdoms—had his son Jeroboam marry one of Ahab's daughters. When Jeroboam ruled in the south, his relative (through Ahab) Ahaziah was king of Israel.

Jehu killed both of them and the entire house of Ahab. In 841 BC, King Jehu was anointed king of Israel, but the zeal he had toward others, in regard to the idols they worshiped, was not present in his own life. He continued to worship the golden calves. Jehu is depicted on the Black Obelisk that commemorates Shalmaneser III. Jehu, of the house of Omri, is depicted bowing at the feet of Shalmaneser paying tribute. The Black Obelisk is the most complete Assyrian Obelisk and is the earliest ancient depiction of a Biblical character. Some scholars believe this is a depiction of Jeroboam. In either event, we see that Israel is paying tribute to Assyria long before the Assyrians lay siege to Samaria.

The Lord began to "cut short Israel" (**2 Ki. 10:32-33**). In **2 Kings 8:12**, Elisha saw this happening; the instrument God used for His judgment was Hazael of Syria (842—796 BC). Hazael took the land of Gilead, the Gadites and the Ruebenites, and the Manassites from Aroer to Gilead and Bashan.

Athaliah (842—837 BC), the mother of Ahaziah, killed all her grandchildren and destroyed all the royal seed to gain the throne of Judah (**2 Ki. 11:1-2**). One descendant of David survived—Joash—because he was hidden in the temple for six years. After six years, the High Priest engineered for Joash to be proclaimed king and for Athaliah to be killed. During

Joash's reign, Hazael (the king of Syria) successfully attacked Jerusalem and Joash was forced to pay him tribute.

Shamsi-Adad (823—811 BC). In 2 Kings 13:1-9, Assyria invaded Babylon in 814 BC. This was during the reign of Jehoahaz, and during this same time period, Syria oppressed Israel. In 2 Kings 13:4-5, in response to Jehoahaz' call to the Lord for deliverance, Israel is delivered. Assyrian activity in the area stopped Hazael (king of Syria) from completely destroying the kingdom of Israel.

King Joash (835—796 BC) visited the dying prophet, Elisha (2 Ki. 13:14-20). At this time, Joash receives a prophecy telling him that he would have victory over the Syrians three times. The fulfillment of that prophecy is recorded in 1 Kings 13:25. Under King Amaziah, local wars continued: Judah attacked Israel and suffered severe losses.

Adad-nirari (810—783 BC) led campaigns against the Medes, Syria, and Israel. Shalmaneser IV (782—772 BC) successfully defended against attacks from the east, but lost most of Syria. Ashur-dan III (772—755 BC) was hit by a plague in 765 BC, a revolt in 763 BC (which lasted until 759 BC). When hit by another plague, it resulted in a political decline that lasted during the time of Ashur-nirari V (755—745 BC). After so many national disasters, it is understandable that the people of Nineveh would be open to hear from a foreign prophet.

It was during this period in Assyrian history that Jonah received his call to Nineveh (750 BC). Nineveh was located at the junction of the Tigris and Khasr Rivers between the Mediterranean Sea and the Indian Ocean. Jonah was, no doubt, a popular prophet as his prophecies were foretelling restoration of territory (2 Ki. 14:25). He was a Galilean and that is interesting in regard to **John 7:52** when the Sanhedrin mistakenly claim "... *out of Galilee ariseth no prophet.*" Jonah was from Gath-hepher which is three miles north of Nazareth.

Tiglath-pileser III (744—727 BC) seized the throne from Ashur-nirari and became the founder of the Second Assyrian Empire. When he seized control, Assyria was in a weakened state. Many of the large provinces were trying to become independent. Babylon was a threat. Tiglath-pileser III subdivided the provinces and appointed Assyrian officials responsible for a professional army funded through tax revenues.

He subjected Syria and Israel, and merged Babylon into the Assyrian Empire. He introduced the policy of transplanting subject population. These forced migrations made the transplants dependent upon their king for protection. From 742 BC to 741 BC, tens of thousands were transplanted.

Syro Ephraim War - 740 BC

Assyria, under the leadership of Tiglath-Pileser III, had regained its power and was once again a threat to the smaller nations. Israel, which is also called Ephraim because of the largest tribe, and Syria, also called Damascus or Aram (both of whom had been tributary nations of Assyria) formed an alliance to oppose the rising power and expansion of Assyria. Judah did not join their alliance, and as a result, was attacked by armies led by Pekah of Israel and Rezin of Syria. Judah, led by Ahaz, lost 120,000 troops in one day and many were taken captive.

During the invasion, the Philistines and the Edomites took advantage of the situation by raiding towns and villages in Judah. Ahaz called out to Tiglath-Pileser III of Assyria for help. The Assyrians defended Judah, conquering Israel, Syria and the Philistines. Ahaz had to pay tribute to Assyria with treasures from the temple in Jerusalem and the royal treasury. He also built idols to Assyrian gods in Judah to find favor with his new ally. Tiglath-Pileser left an inscription recording king Ahaz and his tribute (2 Chr. 28, 2 Ki. 16:1-18).

Isaiah Prophesies

During the Syro-Ephraimite War

The Immanuel child prophecy of the book of Isaiah is closely related to the Syro-Ephraimite war. **Isaiah 7:1-13** states that the kings will be unsuccessful and tells Ahaz to ask God for a sign. He refuses, claiming he does not want to test God (Dt. 6:16). Isaiah, then, announces that God Himself will give the sign: A young woman shall conceive and bear a son, and shall call his name Immanuel (God with us). He shall eat curds and honey when he knows how to refuse the evil and choose the good. For the child knows how to refuse the evil and choose the good, the land before whose two kings you dread will be deserted (Isa. 7:14-16 RSV). The significance of this is that Assyria will not overtake Judah because God is with them. Ahaz's refusal to believe the prophet will lead Assyria directly to the gates of Judah.

The next chapter (Isa. 8) details another prophecy about a child by the name of Maher-shalal-hash-baz (quick to plunder, speedy to spoil). Isaiah, then, explains the significance of this name—that before this child can speak, Assyria will plunder both Syria and Ephraim. Isaiah concludes these prophecies concerning his children (Shear-Jashub—meaning remnant returns, Isa. 7:3), Immanuel (God with us) and Maher-shalal-hash-baz, meaning quick to plunder) by saying "Here I am and the children the LORD has given me. We are signs and symbols in Israel from the LORD Almighty, who dwells in Mount Zion" (Isa. 8:18 NIV).

Israel - Northern Kingdom

In 2 Kings 17:3-6, we find Shalmaneser V (726—721 BC) taking punitive action against Israel in a campaign to quell the rebellion of King Hoshea. It seems that Hoshea was attempting to enlist Egypt's help in rebelling against Assyria. Shalmaneser laid a three-year siege on Samaria, but died shortly before the city was captured. The credit for the victory went to his successor, Saragon II, in 722 BC. An Assyrian cuneiform claims that 27,290 captives were carried away from Samaria. They were never given an edict with permission to return and have become known as the ten lost tribes of Israel (1 Chr. 5:26)

Ten Northern Tribes

It has been said that God never "lost" anyone. Therefore, the ten tribes of the north are not lost to Him. There is evidence that some of the northern tribes were still around at the time of Jesus with their identity intact. In **Luke 2:36**, there is reference to "... *Ana, a prophetess, the daughter of Phanuel of the tribe of Asher* ... " Asher was a tribe of the northern kingdom of Israel.

2 Chronicles 30:1 tells us that when Hezekiah reinstated the Passover that he wrote letters also to *"Ephraim and Manasseh that they should come to the house of the Lord at Jerusalem ..."* And in the same chapter of **2 Chronicles 30** in **verse 11**, Zebulon is listed as humbling themselves and coming to Jerusalem. Also in **verse 18**, it is recorded that Issachar with Zebulon kept the Passover in Jerusalem. Some scholars believe that there were many from the northern tribes who came to Jerusalem to keep the feasts and remained there. That is one likely possibility. Another possibility, which is plausible, is that when Assyria attacked the north many refugees fled to Judah.

In **Ezra 2:70**, it lists "... *and all [of] Israel in their cities*". This verse was written after the seventy years of Babylonian captivity. When the first group of exiles returned to the land under Zerubbabel, all of Israel is mentioned as living in their cities. In **Revelation 7: 4-8**, it states that 144,000 are sealed of *all the tribes of Israel.* The verses (in Revelation that follow) lists each tribe.

Samaritans

Assyria repopulated Samaria with peoples of foreign lands which they had conquered (**2 Ki. 17:24**). The Lord sent lions among them and the people complained to Assyria that they did not know the God of this land and therefore did not know how to please him. So, one of the priests that they had carried away came and lived in Bethel and instructed them in the fear of the Lord. This, of course, was a priest from the idol worshipping northern kingdom (**2 Ki. 17:25-28**). These people became the Samaritans mentioned in the New Testament and were loathed by the Jews.

Prophets: Amos, Isaiah, and Hosea

Sennacherib (704—681 BC)

Sennacherib made Nineveh his capital. He built a new palace, beautified the city, and erected inner and outer walls around the city. During his reign, he faced a problem with Babylon where the growth and power of the Chaldean and Aramean tribes was disrupting the commerce of the urban centers. The trade routes were no longer safe. Elam interfered and worsened the problem.

Between 703 BC and 689 BC, Sennacherib led six campaigns. In 703 BC, the Chaldeans, led by Marduk-apla-iddina II—and supported by the Arameans and the Elamites—rebelled against Assyria. In 701 BC, Egypt instigated a rebellion that was backed by Merodach-Baladan (who was Chaldean), and the rebellion broke out in Judah. Sennacherib reacted firmly to this rebellion taking cities in Judah but not Jerusalem. The Chaldeans again rebelled and were defeated four more times during the period of 694 BC through 689 BC. It would only be a matter of time before a new empire would rule.

Judah

Hezekiah began his reign over Judah in 714 BC. He repaired the temple and reorganized the services. He also reinstated the pilgrimages for Passover and abolished idol worship as recorded in the book of **2 Chronicles 29-31**. Hezekiah even sent letters of invitation to the remaining northern tribes inviting them to participate in the Passover.

Hezekiah made an alliance with Egypt and stopped paying tribute to Assyria. He was expecting Egypt to come to the aid of Judah when Assyria attacked. Egypt did not aid Judah. **Isaiah 30-31, 36:6-9** records the prophet's message concerning trusting men and horses. Sennacherib did attack in response to this rebellion, and Hezekiah had to pay 300 talents of silver and 30 talents of gold (**2 Ki. 18:13-16**). Assyrian records state that the siege was lifted after Hezekiah acknowledged his mistake. It is recorded in Assyrian accounts that Sennacherib took 46 cities and 200 captives.

Sennacherib later sent certain men to threaten attack on Judah (2 Ki. 18:17-37), but the prophet Isaiah promises Hezekiah that God will protect him. In preparation for this attack, Hezekiah built the Broad Wall and a tunnel to carry water into the city. This tunnel is still in Jerusalem, and I have walked through it! It was a remarkable engineering accomplishment. Sennacherib's army arrived and encamped around the walled cities intending to take them. However, the Lord responded to Hezekiah's prayer, and the Lord sent an angel who killed 185,000 Assyrians (2 Chr. 32:1-23).

After this, Hezekiah was taken ill. The prophet Isaiah received a word from the Lord that He would extend his life for fifteen years. When Berodach-baladan (the son of Baladan, the king of Babylon) heard that Hezekiah had been sick and had recovered, he sent a present to him. Hezekiah showed him all the wealth in Jerusalem. Consequently, Isaiah the Prophet went to Hezekiah and asked about the men and what Hezekiah had shown them. Isaiah then gave a prophecy that Babylon would carry away all that was laid in store in Jerusalem (2 Ki. 20, Isa. 39).

Esarhaddon (680—689 BC) became king of Assyria, and during his reign, he freed the exiles and rebuilt Babylon. His focus was on the Medes against whom he campaigned in 676 BC. In 675 BC, Elam made peace with the Assyrians. Also, occupying his attention was a war from 679 BC to 671 BC during which he conquered the Taurus Mountains. Esarhaddon also conquered Egypt in 671 BC, naming himself "the king of Egypt". During this time, a portion of his army remained in Tyre and Ashkelon.

Ashurbanipal (688—627BC), the last strong king of Assyria, is called Asenappar in the Bible (Ezra 4:10). During his reign, he was involved in military activity against Elam—who had previously made peace with the Assyrians—and he continued to have problems on his borders. From 667 BC to 664 BC, he again fought Egypt (Esarhaddon, his father had conquered Egypt in 671 BC), and he placed a pro-Assyrian ruler in the Nile Delta. His reign marks the end of the great Assyrian kings according to some scholars.

Shamash-shum-ukin (667—648 BC), the brother of Ashurbanipal, reigned as Viceroy of Babylon. In 652 BC, Shamash-shum-ukin revolted with the support of the Elamites, kings of the Sealands, the Chaldean, Merodach-Baladan and the tribes of southern Mesopotamia, (Guti, Amrru, Meluhha) and the Arabs. The Assyrian army invaded and conquered Elam and Babylon.

Nabopolassar (625—605 BC), played a key role in the demise of the Assyrian Empire. He revolted and took the title "king of Babylonia". Assyria was weakened and unable to resist the alliances of the Chaldean and Medes. When the Assyrian capital of Nineveh was overrun by the Babylonians in 612 BC, the Assyrians moved their capital to Harran. When Harran was captured in 610 BC, the capital was once again moved, this time to Carchemish on the Euphrates River. Egypt was allied with the Assyrians and marched in 609 BC to aid the Assyrians against the Babylonians.

Josiah – 673 BC

During Josiah's reign, Pharaoh Necho of Egypt went up to fight with the Assyrians against the Babylonians at Carchemish by the river Euphrates. It was necessary for the Pharaoh's army to pass through Judah. King Josiah went out against him, and Necho sent ambassadors to him explaining that this was not his battle and that Egypt was not coming against Judah. However, Josiah ignored the warning—he fought with Necho and delayed the Egyptian forces in the valley of Megiddo. Josiah was critically wounded and after being returned to Jerusalem, he died (2 Ki. 23 and 2 Chr. 35:20-27).

The Egyptians and Assyrians together crossed the Euphrates and laid siege to Harran—which they failed to retake. The

Egyptians met the full might of the Babylonian army led by Nebuchadnezzar at Carchemish where the combined Egyptian and Assyrian forces were destroyed. Assyria ceased to exist as an independent power, and Egypt retreated and was no longer a significant force.

The prophet Nahum foretold the fall of Nineveh, which occurred in 612 BC. Nineveh was surrounded by sixty miles of wall, three walls deep. Within, there were pastures for cattle and fields for crops. They were able to withstand a five year siege. So complete was the devastation by the Babylonians and the Medes and Scythians that when Alexander the Great marched his army in this area, he didn't even see the remains of the once great city. Because there was no evidence of the once great Nineveh, scholars believed the scriptural account to be a fable. Then in 1820 AD, a mound (also called a *"tel"* which indicates an ancient civilization is buried beneath) on the ancient site was discovered and surveyed. Archeologists uncovered the ruins of ancient Nineveh 2,432 years after its destruction.

Jehoiakim

Defeated, the Pharaoh Necho took Jehoahaz, Josiah's son, to Egypt and placed Eliakim on the throne, changing his name to Jehoiakim. He reigned for eleven years (**2 Chr. 36:1-3**). After three years, Jehoiakim rebelled against Nebuchadnezzar the king of Babylon—probably at the instigation of Egypt. Following Jehoiakim's defeat, as written in **2 Kings 24:7**, *"And the king of Egypt came not again any more out of his land: for the king of Babylon had taken from the river of Egypt unto the river Euphrates all that pertained to the king of Egypt."* Following the death of Jehoiakim, Jehoiachin reigned in Judah for three months.

During Jehoiachin's brief reign, Nebuchadnezzar besieged Jerusalem. The royal family, the princes and the officers, the mighty men and "all of Jerusalem" were taken to Babylon (**2 Ki. 24:14**). Only the poorest of the people remained in the land.

Nebuchadnezzar also took all the vessels of gold from the temple. The king of Babylon made Mattaniah king and changed his name to Zedekiah.

Zedekiah

Zedekiah planned an insurrection with Syria, Moab, Ammon, Tyre and Sidon against Babylon. They failed and Nebuchadnezzar once again besieged Jerusalem and took Zedekiah captive. Nebuchadnezzar's captain, Nebuzar-adan, burned the house of the Lord, the king's house, and all the houses of Jerusalem. He and his army also broke down the walls of Jerusalem (**2 Ki. 25:1-21**). There were from 36,000 to 48,000 captives taken to Babylon (**2 Chr. 36**).

Gedaliah ben Ahikam

Two parties formed in the court in Jerusalem—one pro Babylon the other pro Egypt. Gedaliah ben Ahikam was appointed by Nebuchadnezzar to govern. He was murdered by a jealous descendant of the House of David. Those associated with him in government were afraid that Nebuchadnezzar would believe they were responsible, so they escaped to Egypt and forced Jeremiah the Prophet to go with them (**2 Ki. 22:22-26**). In the Upper Nile, the Elephantine Island became a Jewish military colony with a temple. The temple was destroyed in 410 BC and rebuilt in 402 BC.

The Jewish calendar commemorates the anniversary of the murder of Gedaliah with a fast day—because this day marked the final destruction of the Hebrew Commonwealth.

Three Deportations

There were three deportations of the Jews to Babylon. The first was in 597 BC during the reign of Jehoiachin, the second in 587 BC during the reign of Zedekiah, and the final deportation was in 586 BC, following the murder of Gedaliah.

The neighboring nations moved into Judean territory—from the east, the Ammonites, from the south, the Edomites, and from the north, the Samaritans. Seventy years later, these were the nations that opposed Zerubbabel and the first group of returning Jews in their effort to rebuild the temple.

REFERENCES

Bromiley, G. W. (Ed.). (1979). *The international standard Bible encyclopedia*. Grand Rapids, MI: Wm. B. Eerdmans Publishing Company.

Chadwick, H. (1993). *The early Church*. Middlesex, UK: Penguin Books.

Ephraim, S. (Ed.). (1993). *The new encyclopedia of archaeological excavations in the Holy Land*. Jerusalem, IL: The Israel Exploration Society, Carta.

Harrison, R. K. (Ed.). (1988). *The new Unger's Bible dictionary*. Chicago, IL: Moody Press.

Ye'or, B. (1996). *The decline of Eastern Christianity under Islam from Jihad to Dhimmitude*. Cranbury, NJ: Fairleigh Dickinson University Press.

Whiston, W. (1999). *The new complete works of Josephus*. Grand Rapids, MI: Kregel Publications.

CHAPTER EIGHT

BABYLONIAN CAPTIVITY: THE RETURN

DISCUSSION QUESTION: Would the Jews be able to keep the Law in captivity?

From the earliest beginnings of Judaism, when Yahweh called Abram from the Ur of Chaldees, the relationship involved a specific geographical area. A land known then as Canaan and later renamed Israel. During the time of the patriarchs, altars were built to the true and living God, and through their sojourn in Egypt, the hope of returning to the land that Yahweh had promised them was kept alive, as evidenced in Joseph's request that his bones be carried back to the land to be buried. So too, during the first kingdom period of Israel, their relationship with God was intrinsically woven into, and a part of, their residence in the land of Israel.

The religious practices that were observed in the worship of their God took place in the temple which was in Jerusalem. Their sacrifices could only be offered at the temple under the supervision of the priests. Their three major feasts involved pilgrimages to Jerusalem. Worship of Yahweh required the existence of the temple in the city of Jerusalem in the land of Israel. How could the Jews worship their God in a foreign and strange land? The following Psalm expresses that concern:

> "By the rivers of Babylon, there we sat down, yea, we wept, when we remembered Zion . . . For there, they that carried us away captive required of us a song; and they that wasted us required of us mirth, saying, sing us one of the songs of Zion. How shall we sing the Lord's song in a strange land? If I forget thee O Jerusalem, let my right hand forget her cunning. . . "
> (Ps. 137:1-5).

Judaism Prior to Captivity

What were the religious practices of the Jews prior to the captivity? These practices, when observed, were based on the Law of Moses—the Torah. The Sabbath was the first holy day given to God's people (**Gen. 2:3**), "*And God blessed the seventh day and sanctified it; because that in it He had rested from all His work which God created and made.*" Much later in history while in the Sinai, the Lord gave the Ten Commandments, one of which pertained to the Sabbath (**Dt. 5:12-15**).

> "Keep the Sabbath day to sanctify it, as the Lord thy God hath commanded thee. Six days thou shalt labor, and do all thy work; but the seventh day is the Sabbath of the Lord thy God: in it thou shall not do any work, thou, nor thy son, nor thy daughter, nor thy manservant servant, nor thy maidservant, nor thine ox, nor thine ass, nor any of thy cattle, nor thy stranger that is within thy gates; that thy manservant and thy maidservant may rest as well as thou. And remember that thou wast a servant in the land of Egypt, and that the Lord thy God brought thee out from there through a mighty hand and by an stretched out arm; therefore the Lord thy God commanded thee to keep the Sabbath day."

In Exodus 20: 11 it states, "*For in six days the Lord made heaven and earth . . . and rested the seventh day; wherefore, the Lord blessed the Sabbath day, and hallowed it.*" Further direction is given in **Exodus 35:3**, *"Ye shall kindle no fire throughout your habitations upon the Sabbath day."*

So, basically the Sabbath was observed through resting and not building a fire. There was no requirement to attend services in Jerusalem, although in the temple, there were Sabbath day offerings and ritual.

Instructions for the Passover are given first in **Exodus 12**. It was to be celebrated in the first month through the offering of a lamb, followed by a feast which required that the lamb be eaten with bitter herbs and unleavened bread. Once in the land, the *Passover* was one of the three Pilgrim Feasts (**Dt. 16:1-17**). *Shavuot*, which was the Feast of Weeks, began immediately following the Passover. It was marked by free-will sacrifices. *Succoth* was marked by living in "booths". Each of these Pilgrim Feasts was celebrated in Jerusalem and involved sacrifices and temple rituals. The dilemma facing the Jews in Babylon was, "How do we worship Yahweh in a foreign land, without the temple?" Following is a complete list with scriptural references.

Scriptural Observances Listed

- Exodus 12 — Passover
- Exodus 13 — Firstborn
- Exodus 18 — Appointment of Judges
- Exodus 20 — 10 commandments the 4th Shabbath no work/no fire
- Exodus 21 — Relationships and personal responsibility
- Exodus 22 — Restitution/relationships
- Exodus 25-30 — Regarding the tabernacle and priests
- Exodus 34:18-23 — Pilgrim Feasts
- Leviticus 1-16 — Offerings
- Leviticus 17 — Righteous living
- Leviticus 25:8- — Year of Jubilee; Shabbath years; land of Israel

- Pilgrim Feasts: *"Three times you shall keep a feast to me in the year...* (Feast of Unleavened Bread, the Feast of Harvest and the Feast of Ingathering)... *Three times in the year all your males shall appear before the LORD GOD."* (Ex. 23:14-17). These three Pilgrim Feasts are also known as Passover, First Fruits and the Harvest feast. They each have historical and agricultural significance. Passover commemorates the deliverance of the Children of Israel from Egyptian bondage. The Feast of First Fruits (Shavuot) relates to the wheat harvest, and the Harvest Feast (Sukkoth) relates to the general harvest.

Development of Judaism in Captivity

The great advantage for the survival of Jewish identity in Babylon was that they were able to settle in a single place. Unlike Assyria, Babylon did not disperse captives throughout other lands. The exiles were permitted to settle near the Chebar River, where they were able to farm and to engage in other forms of labor. Many Jews became wealthy. And, as we know from the books of Daniel (Ezra, and Nehemiah) some Jews were placed in high positions in the government. In captivity, they became known as "benè gola", children of the exile. In Babylon, they forged a new national identity and a new religion.

In exile, the Jews became accustomed to meeting together on the Sabbath. The Sabbath coincided with the market day which made it convenient. During these meetings, a portion of the Torah and the Prophets were recited. This became firmly established in Judaism. In the land of Israel before the captivity, Jews did not meet on the Sabbath. If they were observant Jews, they rested in their own homes. In captivity, the Sabbath became a Day of Assembly and this was a major change in Judaism.

Other Days of Assembly included the feasts. At these assemblies, they would sing the songs that had accompanied the sacrifices for the particular feast or holy day. If there was a prophet in attendance, he would address the people. The scribes would read a portion of the Torah. There were few prophets in exile and the scribes slowly rose as leaders. The scribe's were a body of teachers whose office it was to interpret the law to the people. They established schools and wrote prayers. The chief of the scribes was Ezra, and the organization of the scribes began with him and ended with Simon the Just. There is mention of an Ezra and the scribes' role in **Nehemiah 8:8-9**, "*So they read in the book in the law of God distinctly, and gave the sense, and caused them to understand the reading . . . and Ezra, the priest, the scribe, and the Levites who taught the people . . .*"

In the early stages in Babylon, the scribe's main interest was in preserving the old literature of the Hebrews. They collected these writings and made them available for the exiles to read. Gradually, they became involved in the explanation of how to keep the Law. They eventually took the place of the prophets and further developed the interpretation of the law as a means for the Jews to practice their religion without access to the temple.

The role of the scribes as interpreters of the Law was a major change in Judaism. There were other major changes in the religious life, such as observing fast days for the day the walls of Jerusalem began to crumble and for the day Jerusalem fell. These additions to their observances and the writings of the scribes were the beginnings of what today is known as the Talmud. Included in the Talmud is the Oral Law, which is a legal commentary on the Torah which explains how the 613 laws of Moses are to be carried out, and the *Mishna*, which is the codification of the oral law into 63 tractates. Thus, the Babylonian captivity had a tremendous impact on how Judaism came to be practiced. It is worth mentioning also that in Babylon, the current Hebrew script was adopted, and the canonization of the Bible was begun.

During the Babylonian captivity, the focus of Judaism shifted from animal sacrifices to the study of the Torah. This gave rise to *professional clergy*—the rabbi. A rabbi is a scholar and a teacher who is responsible to explain God's expectations to the common people.

Prophets in Exile

Ezekiel was a priest and a prophet. He was taken into exile by Nebuchadnezzar along with king Jehoiachin as well as 10,000 of the leaders and skilled craftsmen of Judah (**2 Ki. 24:8-17**). Prior to the exile, Ezekiel had a few visions of the corruption at the temple, the coming invasion and the final fall of Jerusalem, but other than that, his entire ministry was in Babylon. While his early visions were of the destruction of Jerusalem, the later prophecies are of the future restoration of Israel.

Daniel was of royal lineage and was also carried into captivity with Jehoiachin. He took a strong, uncompromising stand for God, and as a result, the Lord used him greatly. He served as a high official in Babylon under the following kings: Nebuchadnezzar, Evil-Merodach, Nergal-sharezer, Labashi-Marduk, Nabonidus, and Belshazzar. After the fall of Babylon to the Persians, he served Darius the Mede.

Babylonian Empire

Evil-Merodach (Amel-Marduk) reigned from 561 BC to 560 BC. He released Jehoiachin from prison and elevated him above the other kings who were captives (**2 Ki. 25:27-30**). Nergal-sharezer (559—556BC) married the daughter of Nebuchadnezzar and murdered her brother Evil-Merodach to take the throne. Nergal-sharezer is mentioned as one of the princes who came against Judah (**Jer. 39:3**). His son, Labashi-Marduk, followed him as king but was assassinated nine months after his inauguration. Nabonidus, the next king, was followed by Belshazzar of the book of Daniel. He was the last of the Babylonian kings as the empire was taken over by the Persians.

Medo-Persia Empire

After seventy years, in which there were six different kings and two empires, the Jews began their return to the land. There were three returns, just as there were three deportations. The first return was under Zerubbabel, the second under Ezra, and the final return under Nehemiah.

The Return:
Zerubbabel - Cyrus 538—520 BC

The Jews prospered in Babylon, so much so, that when Zerubbabel led the first group of 48,360 back to Jerusalem, it represented only a small percentage of the Jewish population in Persia. The book of Ezra opens with the Lord stirring up King Cyrus to proclaim that the God of heaven had charged him with building a house for Him in Jerusalem. He exhorted the Jews to return, but realizing not all would return, he instructed those who remained to provide for those going. Two hundred years earlier, the Lord had called Cyrus by name in the book of Isaiah (Isa. 48:28, 45:1). These prophetic scriptures no doubt motivated King Cyrus in this manner.

This is the first of three "returns" to Jerusalem. The journey took between four to six months and covered nine hundred miles. After arriving in Jerusalem, they rebuilt the altar and worship was re-established. There was local opposition to the Jews rebuilding Jerusalem. After receiving a letter of complaint concerning the Jews, king Artaxerxes demanded that the work cease. This cessation lasted for between sixteen and eighteen years until Haggai the Prophet challenged them to continue to do the work of the Lord.

Esther - Ahasuerus (Xerxes I) 486—465 BC

The book of Esther records that Xerxes's reigned from India to Ethiopia and that he was hosting a feast for all his princes and his servants. This feast probably lasted for six months. Since he would not have called all his princes and servants together at one time (that would have left parts of his empire vulnerable), it is believed that the purpose for entertaining his officials was to persuade them to go to war against the Greeks.

The Battle of Salamis was fought during this war. The Persian navy confronted the Greek city-states in the straights between the mainland and the island of Salamis. The Greeks were victorious and King Xerxes returned to Persia, leaving his army and navy to continue the war against the Greeks. It is probably upon his return to Persia that he began his search for a new queen. The Greeks were victorious again over the Persian army and navy.

The cost of this war would have been great, and it is possible Xerxes raised Haman up to such a high position in his administration because he was a wealthy man. Haman, the Agagite, was a descendant of king Agag (whom Saul failed to kill), an ancient enemy of the Jews with resources to cause them much harm. In **Esther 3:9**, Haman offers 10,000 talents of silver to be paid into the king's treasury for the destruction of the Jews. The annual income for the king's treasury was 15,000 talents of silver. His plans for destruction returned on Haman's own head, and the Jews in Persia continued to prosper.

Ezra

Artaxerxes (Cambyses) 530—521 BC, **Ezra 4-6**
Pseudo-Smerdis (Artaxerxes) 521 BC, **Ezra 4:7-23**
Darius the Great 521—486BC, **Ezra 5-6**

<u>Xerxes (Ahasuerus) 486—465 BC, Esther</u>
<u>Artaxerxes II 464—425 BC, Ezra 7-10</u>

Ezra led the second group of Jews to return to Jerusalem. This was a much smaller group of only a couple thousand, and there were no Levites among them. After about eight days at the river that runs to *Ahava* (a tributary to the Euphrates), Ezra evidently stopped to reorganize. At this point, he discovered there were no Levites among them.

The Levites were dependent on the tithes from the congregation for their support, and evidently did not like the prospects of doing so in Jerusalem. They were comfortable, and even prosperous in Persia. Jerusalem was a city that was in shambles; the economy would not be prosperous and life would be difficult. The Levites opted to remain in the comfort of captivity.

Ezra sent a message back to the Iddo, the chief at Casiphia, demanding that they send to them "ministers for the house of our God". Two hundred and fifty eight Levites were then sent to join them (**Ezra 8:15-21**).

When Ezra arrived in Jerusalem, he found that "... *the people of Israel, and the priests, and the Levites have not separated themselves from the people of the lands ...* " Ezra chapter nine deals with these "abominations"—and continuing on in chapter ten—it took Ezra and the appointed judges three months to process all of these mixed marriages. Note in **Ezra 10:18** that the priests are listed as having taken *strange* wives. This intermarriage of the priestly line will occur again in Nehemiah's time and throughout Jewish history to the time of Jesus.

Artaxerxes II 464—425 BC - Nehemiah 2
Darius II - Nehemiah 12:22

Nehemiah led the third group of Jews returning to Jerusalem during the reign of Artaxerxes. Some scholars believe that the mention of the queen in **Nehemiah 2:6** is a reference to Queen Esther, and that the king at the time was her husband. Others believe that this Artaxerxes was her stepson. The king not only granted permission to return to Jerusalem, but gave him all that was needed for a safe journey, and the timber that would be used to build the gates of the city (**Neh. 2:7-9**).

Upon Nehemiah's arrival, he encountered three characters that would persistently attempt to prevent the rebuilding of the walls of Jerusalem. These enemies are known as Sanballat, the governor of Samaria (north), also known as Sanballat the Horonite, Tobiah the Ammonite (east), and Geshem the Arab (south). In **Nehemiah 4:7**, the Ashdodites (west) are also listed. Jerusalem was totally surrounded by enemies.

When the rebuilding of the wall began, Eliashib, the priest, was one of the first to begin the work (**Neh. 3:1**). Yet, years later when Nehemiah returns again to Jerusalem, Eliashib has prepared a place for the enemy in a chamber of the house of God. Eliashib allied himself with Tobiah (**Neh. 13:1-9**). In addition, Eliashib had allowed his grandson to marry into the family of Sanballat (**Neh. 13:28**). According to Josephus, this expelled grandson of Eliashib became the chief priest of the Samaritan temple built by Sanballat on Mt. Gerizim. The Samaritans remain until this day, and each year they celebrate Passover on Mt. Gerizim.

Summary

The removal of God's chosen people from the land He had given them began with the Assyrian's capture of the northern kingdom (722 BC). The Assyrian policy was to divide the conquered peoples and use them to repopulate other lands they had conquered. Thus, the ten tribes of the northern kingdom were dispersed throughout the Assyrian empire. There were, however, representatives of these tribes who had escaped to Judah, so there is no basis for the idea of the ten lost tribes.

Judah was conquered by Babylon (586 BC), whose policy it was to allow conquered people to remain together and to develop within their own communities. Therefore, the Jews in the Babylonian captivity were able to prosper and to create a new religious identity. The scribes took the place of the prophets and became the religious leaders and teachers.

The Medo-Persian Empire had a policy of allowing conquered people to return to their lands (539—464 BC). Under the leadership of Zerubbabel, Ezra, Nehemiah and thousands of Jews returned to Jerusalem. This begins the Second Temple period in Jewish history. Persia was still a ruling empire at the beginning of the Second Temple period but hovering on the horizon were the Greeks—who Xerxes had failed to conquer. The Greeks presented the next great challenge to Judaism.

ଓଃ

REFERENCES

Bromiley, G. W. (Ed.). (1979). *The international standard Bible encyclopedia.* Grand Rapids, MI: Wm. B. Eerdmans Publishing Company.

Ephraim, S. (Ed.). (1993). *The new encyclopedia of archaeological excavations in the Holy Land.* Jerusalem, IL: The Israel Exploration Society, Carta.

Grayzel, S. (1984). *A history of the Jews: From the Babylonian exile to the present 5728-1968.* New York, NY: Meridian.

Mazar, A. (1992). *Archaeology of the land of the Bible 10,000-586 B.C.E.* New York, NY: Doubleday.

Snell, D. C. (1997). *Life in the Ancient Near East, 3100-332 B.C.E.* New Haven, CT: Yale University Press.

Whiston, Wm. (1999). *The new complete works of Josephus.* Grand Rapids, MI: Kregel Publications.

CHAPTER NINE

SECOND TEMPLE PERIOD

DISCUSSION QUESTION: What did so many from the priestly line remain in Babylon?

Judaism Transformed

The Jews that returned to Israel lived primarily in Judea. They were mostly farmers or peasants. Under Zerubbabel, Ezra, and Nehemiah, the temple had been rebuilt, and worship was reestablished. As a vassal state under a foreign power—namely the Persian Empire, the Jews were not permitted to have a king. The High Priest was directly accountable to the Persian king to maintain order, collect taxes, and ensure loyalty to the empire. In effect, the High Priest replaced the role of king. The High Priest's duties, as ordained by God, were confined to matters of worship; under this system, it became a political position.

There were no more prophets after Malachi until John the Baptist. The scribes replaced the prophets. Prophets were given direct revelation from God and were used to encourage, to exhort and to teach God's people. The scribes, on the other hand, encouraged knowledge, created literature, and formulated laws. From the Law and the Prophets, they derived those ideas which were to guide the people—the laws of men. Jewish life was transformed as a result of teaching and interpretation.

The scribes taught in the community houses which were centrally located in every community. Community houses are better known by the Greek name synagogue. Synagogues became a part of Judaism during the exile. In exile, the Jews developed the tradition of meeting together on the Sabbath and on Holy Days. At these gatherings a portion of the Torah and the Prophets were recited. This became a firmly established part of Judaism. The government was also administered from the Community House. Within a century of Nehemiah's time, the scribes and the synagogues had become tremendously influential. There is an expression in Judaism. . . *"Generals and statesmen decided the fate of other peoples; writers and teachers molded the destiny of the Jews"*. Those writers and teachers were the scribes.

To get a better understanding of what that expression means, let's look at the traditions for keeping the Sabbath that were formulated through the interpretation of the scribes. The Law of Moses mandated a day of rest in which no manner of work was to be done, and no fire was to be built. In exile, this was extended to include the gathering together on the Sabbath. Over time the concept of rest was further interpreted and traditions established that dictated what *rest* entailed. Still further on in history, the command to not build a fire was interpreted as it related to electricity and automobiles.

Rabbis were concerned that no well-intended Jew would ever inadvertently break the Law. This concern was translated into the traditions and became known as the Fence around the Law. The thought was that the Fence protected the Law and ensured that the Jews kept the Law of Moses. For example, to ensure that work is never done on the Sabbath, it is traditionally forbidden to write letters, or to walk more than 3,000 feet (which is considered a Sabbath's Day Journey). To ensure no fire is kindled on the Sabbath, the observant Jew today is not permitted to turn on electric lights, drive a car, or watch TV, and—the list goes on.

There is another expression in Judaism that can be understood in the context of the traditional laws of the Sabbath. It is, *"More than Israel kept the Shabbath, the Shabbath kept Israel"*. An observant Jew could not walk more than 3,000 feet on the Sabbath; therefore, he needed to live within 3,000 feet of the synagogue in order to attend services. In every country throughout the world where Jews settled, the community surrounded a synagogue keeping the Jewish community intact.

After the Jews returned to the land of Israel, while the nation was growing into its new form of government headed by the High Priest, and developing traditions in the keeping of the Law, there were political developments taking place in Persia and in the west which would have a dramatic impact on Israel.

Persia

Artaxerxes III's reign (425—338 BC) coincided with Philip of Macedon (whom we will look at later) and Nectanebo II of Egypt. Bagoas was Artaxerxes III's Chief Minister. When Bagoas fell from favor, he killed most of the sons of Artaxerxes III. The youngest son Arses of Persia, also known as Artaxerxes IV, reigned from 338—336 BC. Bagoas had him murdered and replaced by his cousin Darius III. When Darius III became too independent for Bagoas, he planned to poison him. Darius III was informed of the plan and forced Bagoas to drink the poison himself. The Persian court was filled with internal conflict and intrigue, which greatly weakened them in the face of the upcoming world power in the west.

Macedon-Greece

Macedonia was a Greek state north of Greece. Philip of Macedon was born in 382 BC and rose to power in 359 BC. He died in 336 BC. He was the youngest son of king Amyntas III who was held hostage by the Greeks at Thebes from 368—365 BC. When Philip became king, the kingdom he ruled was divided and under attack. Within a year, he removed the internal threats and secured the safety of the kingdom. After defeating their ancient enemy Illyria, Philip continued on to the Adriatic coast.

With his throne firmly established, Philip concentrated on building his army. The military became professional and were paid well. This enabled them to remain in the service throughout the year—as there was no need to return to their farms to support themselves—as had been the case in the past. His soldiers used a Phalanx formation and Sarissa that enabled them protection through holding their shields tightly touching. The Sarissa was a type of spear that was eighteen feet long (6 meters).

Philip further strengthened his kingdom through marriages. In 357 BC, he married Princess Olympias of Epirus. She bore him a son, Alexander. Of his many wives, Cleopatra was the only one of Macedonian nobility. Cleopatra also bore him a son, and Alexander was then considered an illegitimate heir to the throne since his mother was not a Macedonian.

In the same year that Philip married Olympias, he broke the treaty with Athens and attacked Amphipolis. By 356 BC, his campaign to conqueror Greece was in full force. In 338 BC, he became the Commander of the Greeks following his victory at the Battle of Chaeronea. In 337 BC, tens of thousands of Greeks joined the Persian army rather than come under the authority of a Macedonian. Not deterred in the least by this, Philip began his invasion of Persia in 336 BC but was assassinated in the same year.

Alexander III - Alexander the Great 356—323 BC

Alexander was sent to study with Aristotle, who had previously served in the court of Hermeias in Atarneus. Philip believed this alliance would prove helpful for his plan to invade Persia. Aristotle's father had also served as a physician for an earlier Macedonian king. Thus Aristotle was considered to be an appropriate and beneficial tutor for Alexander. Of the many subjects Alexander studied, he had special interest in medicine and he loved Greek poetry, especially Homer. He studied for three years under Aristotle's *tutelage* before returning at age sixteen to serve as Regent of Macedon and Master of the Royal Seal while his father was directly involved in battle.

The favored son of Philip and Cleopatra was not old enough to take the throne in 336 BC following Philip's assassination. Thus, Alexander succeeded his father. He immediately ordered the execution of all his enemies. He acted swiftly to squelch rebellions throughout his kingdom including the Greek rebellion—during which Alexander devastated the Thebes (where his grandfather had been held hostage). He then assigned Antipater as regent and focused on the battle with Persia.

When Alexander took command, the invasion of Persia was already set in motion. Darius III was on the throne and joining his army were 30,000 Greeks. Alexander defeated Darius at the Battle of Issus and this opened the way for his army to conquer Syria and Phoenicia. In 331 BC, he entered Egypt. Here, the city of Alexandria was built on the Nile and named after him.

Alexander the Great at Jerusalem

In 329 BC, Simon the Just was High Priest, and he was no doubt concerned about the growing threat of Alexander. Simon decided to accommodate rather than attempt to fight Alexander. In the Talmud (Yoma 69a), their first encounter is described. Simon came forth from Jerusalem with many priests and sages from the Sanhedrin to greet Alexander at the gates of Jerusalem. Alexander got off his horse and bowed to Simon. When questioned about this by his officers, Alexander said that every time he went into battle he had a dream of an angel leading him. The face of Simon the Just was the face of the angel in his dreams. Alexander granted the Jews autonomy. The only requirement was the payment of taxes and sworn loyalty. The Jews, in response and appreciation to Alexander's generosity, named every child born, during the following year, Alexander. This opened the door for other Greek names and ultimately the adoption of the Greek language.

Alexander did not have a vision of uniting all the conquered peoples into one empire but rather into one cultural unity. He wanted to combine the philosophy and literature of Greece with the wealth and grandeur of Persia. He built new cities and enlarged old ones. He encouraged Greeks to settle there and to teach the local population how to live like Greeks.

Israel

Israel was now ruled by the powers of the west. Trade and commerce came from the west and a slow emigration began among the Jewish population. They immigrated to other countries along the Mediterranean, to the Greek Islands, and along the shores of the Black Sea. Greek was the international language and, through the study of Greek, the Jews entered into the Hellenization (from *Hellas* which is the Greek word for *Greece*) process and the adoption of Greek customs.

It is interesting to note that the Sons of Tobias were the principal advocates of the Hellenization. This family could be traced back to Tobias the Ammonite who, in the book of Nehemiah, is listed as the chief opponent to the rebuilding of the wall of Jerusalem. Subsequently, the family identified themselves with the Jews and intermarried with the family of the high priest. They became members of the High Council and played an important role in government. Joseph ben Tobias bought the right to collect taxes from all of Syria (Israel was designated as a part of the Syrian province by the foreign powers that ruled) and in so doing, he became a great economic force in Jerusalem.

Alexandria

An example of how comfortable Jews were living outside of Israel can be found in Alexandria. It was a city named after

Alexander the Great and planned by Ptolemy, one of his generals. It was a commercial port-city populated with Greeks and peoples from conquered areas. From the beginning, Jews were a part of this city and eventually became an important part of the Alexandrian community. By the third generation, the Jews' mother tongue was Greek and for the most part they only had a minimal understanding of Hebrew and Aramaic. Citizenship in a Greek city required participation in religious practices. The Jews excluded themselves from full citizenship and lived in their own communities (which would not have extended beyond a Sabbath's day journey from their synagogue).

It was in Alexandria that the Septuagint was written. *Septuagint* means *seventy* in Greek, however there were seventy-two who worked on the translation. The translation of the Hebrew Scriptures into Greek took place between 300—200 BC. It was a tremendous undertaking and there was a great celebration upon its completion. Legend has it that the day it was completed was declared an annual holiday. If, however, that was true, we would be better able to pinpoint the exact date.

Conclusion

In conclusion, after the return of the Jews to Israel, the everyday practice of Judaism was completely transformed. The High Priest was the political leader and the scribes became the authority on the interpretation of the Law. The traditional practice of Judaism centered on the *fence around the Law*, which was established by scribes and rabbis to protect the Law.

Following the conquest of Alexander the Great, Jews became *Hellenized* and began to immigrate to other countries. This is the first time in history that Jews willingly left Israel. Strong Jewish communities were developed in Alexandria, and within the boundaries of Babylon and Persia, by the Jews who chose to remain there. Additionally there were smaller and less influential Jewish communities throughout the Greek world.

Upon the death of Alexander the Great, his empire was divided between his two generals since there was no heir apparent. The southern kingdom was led by Ptolemy and the northern by Seleucus. This brings us to the time of the Maccabees.

☙

REFERENCES

Bahat, D. (1996). *The illustrated atlas of Jerusalem*. Jerusalem, ISR: Carta.

Bromiley, G. W. (Ed.). (1979). *The international standard Bible encyclopedia*. Grand Rapids, MI: Wm. B. Eerdmans Publishing Company.

Grayzel, S. (1984). *A history of the Jews from the Babylonian exile to the present 5728-1968*. New York, NY: Meridian.

Harrison, R.K. (Ed.) (1988). *The new Unger's Bible dictionary*. Chicago, IL: Moody Press.

Richman, C. (1997). *A house of prayer for all nations: The holy temple of Jerusalem*. Jerusalem, IL: The Temple Institute, Carta.

Sarel, B. (1997). *Understanding the Old Testament: An introductory atlas to the Hebrew Bible*. Jerusalem, IL: Carta.

Whiston, W. (1999). *The new complete works of Josephus*. Grand Rapids, MI: Kregel Publications.

CHAPTER TEN

SELEUCIDS, PTOLEMIES and MACCABEES

DISCUSSION QUESTION: What are Hellenized Jews?

Upon the death of Alexander the Great (323 BC), his empire was divided between his four generals. The two generals in the east were Seleucus and Ptolemy. Seleucus gained control of Asia and his descendants became known as the Seleucids. Ptolemy gained control of Egypt and his descendants became known as the Ptolemies. Each claimed Israel as part of their kingdom because of its strategic location. This was the beginning of what is known as the Wars of Diadochi in 323 to 305 BC. Thus, once again, Israel became a battle ground caught in the middle of the quest for power by surrounding nations.

By this time, the upper classes of Jerusalem and the chief families among the priests had capitalized on the Greek influence and had become exporters, importers, and merchants. They thought in terms of economic prosperity—having a vision of making Jerusalem a great trading center—by capturing the trade of the caravans from the international highways which ran through Israel to reach Egypt in the south or Damascus in the north. These *upper classes* constantly associated with Greeks and encouraged Jews to dress like Greeks, to participate in the Greek games, and to reorganize the politics of Jerusalem around the Greek constitution.

Rome on the Rise

Rome had been on the move since their revolt in 509 BC against the Etruscans (ancient Italy and Corsica). By 290 BC, they controlled the entire Peninsula of Italy which allowed them to dominate the Mediterranean Sea, bringing them trade and wealth. Ptolemy IV Philometor (181—145 BC) fled to Rome when challenged by his younger brother Euergetes. Rome awarded him Egypt and Cyprus. Alexandria appealed to Rome during Antiochus' invasion of Egypt. Rome was irrevocably involved in Egypt by the time of the Maccabean revolt in Israel.

Hellenized Jews

The Seleucids wanted to reunite all of Alexander's conquests under their control. Antiochus III (198 BC) forced Egypt to give up Israel. Among the Jews, there developed two political parties—those who favored the Seleucids and those who wanted Israel to remain a part of Egypt. Hyrcanus, the son of Joseph ben Tobias, was the tax official for Egypt and favored the Egyptians. His brother and other wealthy men favored the Seleucids (referred to as Syria).

The pro-Syrian faction was seeking favor with Seleucus IV, who was planning to continue his conquests and to take Egypt. They revealed to Seleucus IV that Egypt had money stored in the temple. There were no banks at that time and temples were used to store wealth. Seleucus sent Heliodorus to confiscate the wealth of Egypt in the temple in Jerusalem, but he was unsuccessful. This marked the defeat of the pro-Syrian group in their first attempt to take control of Judea.

The common Jews had not taken sides nor become involved in the political struggles of the upper echelons in Jerusalem. However, the collaboration of the Hellenized Jews with the Syrians in regard to the money in the temple gave them an awareness that the Hellenized Jews would stop at nothing in pursuit of their goals.

Seleucus IV died and his brother Antiochus IV, who gave himself the name of Epiphanes (visible god), succeeded him. Antiochus IV (Epiphanes) also had the goal of conquering Egypt. In his pursuit of this goal, it was important that he have a loyal Hellenized Jewish population in Israel. A group of Jews came to him with a plan which would speed up this process.

The Hellenized Jews wanted the High Priest Onias removed and his Hellenized brother, Jason, to replace him. If this were accomplished, they could gain control of the council. In return for a large sum of money, Antiochus IV (Epiphanes) promised to give Jerusalem a Greek constitution and the right to coin money, which would help the city to develop commercially. When this plan was carried out, the common people were outraged. This was the first time since the Babylonian exile that a foreign government had interfered with the succession of the priesthood.

The Hellenized Jews were now in full control of the government of Judea. They built gymnasiums within Jerusalem and encouraged young people to make full use of them. The young priests began to neglect their duties to engage in temple sports. The Greek language, Greek names, and the Greek style of dress became fashionable in Jerusalem.

However, the more radical Jews did not feel things were moving along fast enough, so they promised Antiochus IV (Epiphanes) another large sum of money to replace Jason with Menelaus who was not even from the high priestly line. Menelaus sold some of the holy vessels from the temple to raise the money to pay Syria.

Antiochus IV (Epiphanes) became impatient with the Jews that refused to become Hellenized and ordered Judaism to be destroyed. A Syrian army marched into Jerusalem to support Menelaus in implementing this new policy. Orders were given prohibiting the observance of Judaism and a statue of Jupiter was placed in the temple above the altar. The statue bore an obvious resemblance to Antiochus. On the 25th of Kislev in the year 168 BC, pigs were offered as a sacrifice. Many Jews in Jerusalem were killed and those who survived escaped to the hills. The common people known as Hasidim which means *pious*, became more fervent in their worship.

The Hasidim had two choices. They could die fighting or they could die as martyrs. Thousands were martyred and thousands fled to the hills. Those who fought were led by the scribes, they were not experienced in warfare, and in addition to this drawback, they would not fight on the Sabbath.

Mattathias and Sons

In Modin, a town northwest of Jerusalem, there lived observant Jews who were the descendants of the priestly line. The Hashmonaim, or Hasmoneans, were a family of respected priests and lived in Modin. Of these families was a man named Mattathias and he had five sons: Simon, Eliezer, Judah, John and Jonathan. The Syrians marched into Modin and into the marketplace, probably facing the synagogue, where they erected an altar. As a priest and elder, Mattathias was ordered to sacrifice a pig.

No doubt silence fell on the crowd. Not a whisper could be heard as everyone held their breath waiting for Mattathias to respond. Into the silent void stepped a Hellenized Jew requesting permission to offer the sacrifice. Each Jew standing in the marketplace that day knew that following the sacrifice they would be forced to eat the pig and those who refused would be killed. Mattathias—unable to endure the insult and the thought of eating pig—grabbed the sword of the captain of the troops and killed the Hellenized Jew and then killed the captain. The sons of Mattathias and the crowd of Jews descended upon the Syrian army killing them, and then, destroying the altar.

Mattathias shouted above the roar of the victorious crowd, "Whoever is for God, let him come unto me". This was a war cry that echoed throughout the land, over the hills and into the caves; everywhere that Jews were hiding, the words of Mattathias resounded. The common people and the Hasidim joined Mattathias and the revolution was born. Mattathias decided it would be necessary to give up one of the foundational principals of Judaism temporarily in order to fight this guerrilla warfare against Syria—they would fight on the Sabbath!

Judah, the Maccabee, took over the command after the death of his father Mattathias. Judah had his motto inscribed on his banner. "Who is like unto Thee among the mighty O Lord?" The guerrilla warfare, led by Judah, was having an impact, and the Parthian revolt further aided their efforts. Antiochus' attention was focused on the Parthians (the ancient Iran-Arsacid Empire), so he left his regent Lysias to deal with the rebellious Jews. Lysias greatly underestimated the strength of the Maccabees. He sent a small Syrian force augmented with Hellenized Jews and volunteers from neighboring nations to squelch the movement. The Maccabees defeated them and opened the Emmaus road enabling them to enter Jerusalem.

The Maccabean soldiers placed guards around the small remaining Syrian army and proceeded to cleanse the temple and rededicate it for the worship of God. The Talmud relates a story concerning the miracle of the oil. The tradition tells that there was only enough clean oil to burn for one day, but that it miraculously lasted for eight days until the Maccabees were able to provide clean oil. This legend was written by a rabbi with the intent that it would interest the children in the celebration of Hanukkah, which is the holiday that commemorates the Maccabean victory.

Syria retaliated by sending Lysias himself with a large army to Jerusalem. The Jews retreated within the walls of Jerusalem. The city was besieged and Lysias was in hope of starving the Jews into submission. However, news reached him of a large rival army marching against Antioch the capitol of Syria. Lysias was needed in Syria. He was forced to make an offer of peace to the Jews.

The following is the agreement that was reached between the Jews and Syria:
1. Promised withdrawal of all the laws against the observance of Judaism
2. Syria would not interfere in the internal conflicts between the Hasidim and the Hellenized Jews
3. Menelaus be removed as high priest and executed
4. Judah and his followers were not to be punished
5. The walls of Jerusalem were to be razed
6. Syria would appoint a new high priest (a mildly Hellenized one)

This would restore the situation to what it was in the days of Jason. Judah was not in favor of accepting the treaty but was over ruled by the council; he and his followers left the city. Alcimus, the newly appointed high priest, restored power to the old oligarchy. The moderate Hasidim were willing to compromise on political issues if their religion was left alone.

Judah resumed the civil war, but he was again left with a small, poorly supported group. So, with an army of only eight hundred, he faced the Syrian army. Judah was killed. After his death, Simon, Jonathan and John fled to Jordan and continued to be a problem for the Syrians. As the new resistance leader, Jonathan led the Hasmonean band in the continued attacks against the Syrians and the Hellenized Jews. But Jonathan was not the military genius that Judah was—he believed in peaceful negotiations to gain independence.

The Syrians were plunged into a civil war following the death of Antiochus (162 BC). There were two contenders for the throne: Demetrius II and Alexander Balas (who was the adopted son of Antiochus IV and Laodice IV)—both of whom laid claim to the Seleucid throne. Alexander's claim as the heir was recognized by the Senate in Rome and by the Ptolemy of Egypt. Both contenders sought the help of Jonathan.

Alexander appointed Jonathan as high priest and sent him a purple robe and a diadem. This assured the Maccabees the support of the Hasidim. In 153 BC, Jonathan officiated as high priest at the altar, which made him the official head of Judea. Demetrius II fully intended to continue his efforts to take the throne, and he promised to grant Jonathan the right to raise and maintain an army. Demetrius regained the throne in 145 BC. Jonathan became a member of Syrian nobility and his brother Simon-was made governor of the Philistine coast.

Upon the death of Jonathan, Simon was elected "Ruler and High Priest until a true prophet should arise" (140—135 BC). In 139 BC, Simon was in Rome and the Roman Republic Senate recognized the new dynasty. At this time, they were semi-independent. Simon called together an extraordinary assembly and was elected to office. This assembly is known as the Great Assembly. In Jewish history, the assembly with Ezra and Nehemiah to ratify the reforms is considered the First Great Assembly. At the time of Simon's assembly, the Hasidic party was the majority. This was the last Great Assembly. The Sanhedrin (of a later date) developed out of this assembly.

Simon's Great Assembly reorganized the Jewish government, and provided for a council with nationwide representatives to assist the high priests. Simon was an old man when he was elected to office, but he faithfully attended to his high priestly and civil duties until he died in 135 BC. His death marked the end of the heroic age of the Hasmonean struggle—the generation that had fought for 35 years for its principals was dying out.

John Hyrcan (i.e. Hyrcanus), Simon's son, marked a new generation. The Maccabean victory was only a memory—it was not their *experience*. Syria backed John Hyrcan conditionally. He had to recognize himself as a Syrian subject and support the king in his military campaigns. Hyrcan gave up to Syria all the pagan cities except for Jaffa. As soon as Syria was distracted with internal problems, Hyrcan regained the coastal cities. This gave the Jews control over the routes to the port. He also conquered Edom (his interest was in the trade route on the Kings Highway which passed through Edom). Hyrcan forced the Idumeans (Greek for Edomites) to convert to Judaism.

The noble Maccabean period had passed. Judah had won religious freedom; Jonathan had won independence and power. It had been a long hard struggle. The heir to this struggle was the Hasmonean Dynasty which began with Simon. His successor was his son, John Hyrcan. Hyrcan began a policy of expansion and forced conversion to Judaism. This policy of forced conversion would become a thorn in the side of Israel until the time of their Diaspora.

○‍R

REFERENCES

Bahat, D. (1995). *Carta's historical atlas of Jerusalem.* Jerusalem, IL: Carta.

Gilbert, M. (1993). *The Dent atlas of Jewish history (from 2000 BC to the present day).* London, UK: The Orion Publishing Group.

Grayzel, S. (1968). *A history of the Jews: From the Babylonian exile to the present 5728-1968.* New York, NY: Meridian.

Whiston, W. (1999). *The new complete works of Josephus.* Grand Rapids, MI: Kregel Publications.

CHAPTER ELEVEN

HASMONEAN and HERODIAN DYNASTIES: 164—63 BC

DISCUSSION QUESTION: What does it mean to be a Jew?

Simon, the first in the Hasmonean Dynasty, completed the emancipation of Israel. He received recognition from Rome (141 BC) and was confirmed as High Priest, captain and governor making his position hereditary in the Maccabean family until "there should arise a faithful prophet" (**1 Mac. 14:41, 47**). He was able to influence Demetrius to release Judah from the tribute they were paying (**1 Mac. 13:41**). Simon gained control of the port city of Jaffa which gave Israel access to commerce and trade with the west; he also called the Great Assembly which birthed the Sanhedrin. Simon and two of his sons were murdered by his son-in-law, Ptolemy in 135 BC. His life represented the last of the Maccabees. Upon his death, his son John Hyrcan succeeded him.

John Hyrcan (134—104 BC) expanded the borders of Israel and introduced forced conversions of the conquered peoples. During his reign, Antiochus VII, king of Syria, invaded Judea and forced John Hyrcan to pay a large indemnity and tribute. After the death of Antiochus VIII, Syria was once again plagued with internal strife. Hyrcan used this opportunity to annex Shechem and destroy the temple of the Samaritans.

John Hyrcan broke with the tradition of the Maccabees' association with the Hasidim and aligned himself with the Sadducees. John Hyrcan's lasting legacy was the forced conversions of the Edomites.

Aristobulus I (Hebrew name was Judah), John Hyrcan's son, succeeded in 104 BC and reigned for one year. Aristobulus threw his mother and three of his brothers into prison to secure his position, and he killed his brother Antigonus. Aristobulus went to war against Ituraea (located at the base of Mt. Herman—Lk. 3:1) and subjugated a large portion of the population. He forced circumcision and strove to convert those who were conquered.

In 103 BC, Alexander Jannaeus took the throne; he reigned until his death in 76 BC. He extended the territory of Israel and gained control of all the commercial centers and highways. He held the Pharisees in check through armed might. In 89 BC, he waged a war with the Arabs in the south and lost. The general population was not happy with Alexander Jannaeus. They expressed their discontent during the Sukkoth celebration following the defeat by the Arabs. Alexander was officiating as high priest in the temple when the people began pelting him with *etrogim*. The *etrogim* are a kind of citron used in the celebration of Sukkoth. He ordered his soldiers to charge into the crowd, resulting in hundreds of deaths.

The Pharisees sought the help of the Syrian king, and Alexander was forced to flee for his life. The Jews then decided they did not want to be under Syrian rule, so they turned to Alexander. When Alexander was reinstated, he sought out and crucified all those who he claimed were guilty of treason. It is said that there were 800 men crucified by Alexander.

Political Parties

The Pharisees—*parash* (which means to separate or oppose)—were the opposition party. They opposed the expansionist policy. They were the descendants of the Hasidim. They believed that it was Judaism that had saved the Jewish nation. And they believed that Judaism was what made them superior to the pagans surrounding them. Because of this belief, they wanted national life and everything else subordinated to their religion. The Pharisees did not believe in forced conversions, they thought that Judaism should be spread by example. They saw the nation as a means of preserving their religion.

The Pharisees had a liberal interpretation of the Torah. They believed that the Biblical Laws were principals and illustrations of these principals. They were committed to the Oral Law—the tradition handed down by the scribes; they insisted on knowledge and piety in every conceivable act.

Pharisees Taught

1. Each man must become close and in direct contact with God.
2. Knowledge is the road to piety, the constant reading of the sacred books (from Ezra onward the tradition of reading portions of the Torah and the Prophets).
3. Every Jew was represented in the public sacrifice that was offered twice daily in the temple. In accordance with "each man," the Pharisees taught that while each man was not at the temple, he could, none-the-less, participate in the sacrifice by reciting the prayers and psalms which accompanied the sacrifice and by reading from the Torah the description of the sacrifice.
4. To fulfill the commandment "be ye holy", every action should be regulated in accordance to the Biblical command as interpreted by the scribes.

Services: Community Houses-Synagogues

1. A description of the public sacrifice that was going on at the temple was read.
2. Recitation of the Psalms that were being recited in the temple.
3. On Shabbath and Holy Days, reading of the portion of the Bible.

4. Later in the afternoon, there was a shorter service that corresponded with the second public sacrifice.

Sadducees

The Sadducees believed in a strong nation, in territorial expansion, and in being ruled by the aristocracy. They believed that national power had saved the people and their religion and agreed with forcible conversions. They saw in Judaism an instrument for uniting the state and assimilating conquered people. They did not give authority to the *Oral Law* because it was not found in the books of Moses. They also did not believe in an existence after death.

Alexander Jannaeus was aligned with the party of the Sadducees. His successor, Salome Alexandra, did not share Alexander's political view.

Salome Alexandra was the wife of Aristobulus I, and Alexander Jannaeus was her step-son. Upon the death of Aristobulus I, she married Alexander in accordance to Jewish Law, since she was left childless. She succeeded Alexander Jannaeus in 76 BC and reigned until 67 BC. She was the sister of the leader of the Pharisees, and upon taking the throne as Queen; she dismissed the Sadducees and appointed Pharisees to the Sanhedrin. The Sanhedrin was the Counsel of State, the Legislature, and the Supreme Court. The Pharisees sought revenge. There was hatred between the two parties: the Pharisees coming from the Hasidim and the Sadducees coming from the Maccabees through Hyrcan.

While Salome was on the throne, Hyrcan II acted as High Priest. He succeeded his mother to the throne in 67 BC. He was the son of Salome and Alexander Jannaeus, and in 67 BC, he became king and continued as high priest. Within three months, he was deposed by his brother, Aristobulus II, and forced to renounce the throne. Aristobulus II reigned until 63 BC. During this time, Aristobulus II sought refuge with Aretas III king of the Nabateans.

Antipater, an Idumean, persuaded Hyrcan to regain power. Aristobulus, with 50,000 Nabateans, attempted to retake the throne. A long siege ensued and both brothers turned to Rome—as Rome had declared itself a friend to the Jews. The Pharisees, who were sent by the Sanhedrin, also made an appeal to Rome. They wanted to be rid of both brothers so that Judea could return to its ancient constitution with high priest and council.

Rome was in the process of territorial expansion, and Pompey had annexed Syria. He saw in the three delegations the opportunity to further the empire of Rome. Pompey marched on Judea killing 12,000 Jews. He entered the temple and penetrated the Holy of Holies. Judea was incorporated into the Roman province of Syria. Hyrcan II was appointed Ethnarch (ruler of the people of Judea) and restored as high priest in 63 BC. He remained ruler and high priest even after Antipater was made procurator of Judea.

Antigonus, the son of Aristobulus II, was the last of the Hasmonean Dynasty. He reigned for three years, from 40 to 37 BC.

It will be helpful to understand the political force that Antipater became before we look at Antigonus.

Herodian Dynasty

Antipater the Idumean, who encouraged Hyrcan II to retake Judea from his brother Aristobulus, became the founder of the Herodian Dynasty. He married Cypros, a Nabatean of a royal family. He became powerful under the Hasmonean kings and subsequently became a client of Rome. Rome placed Antipater in charge of Judea when Julius Caesar and Pompey got into battle in Egypt. Antipater took 3,000 troops and rescued Caesar. For this "demonstration of valor", he was given Roman citizenship. He was ultimately appointed the first Roman Procurator of Judea, laying the foundation for the Herodian Dynasty. Antipater had four sons: Phasael, Herod, Joseph, and Pheroras. He also had a daughter named Salome.

Antipater and Rome were natural allies. The Jews were hostile to both. Antipater began to rebuild the walls of Jerusalem that Pompey had destroyed. He brought a relative calm by threatening to become "a severe master rather than a gentle governor". He became a power broker between the Hasmoneans, the Arabs and the Romans. He appointed his two sons, Phasael and Herod, governors over Jerusalem and Galilee. Hyrcan II was still the ruler and high priest at this time.

The Roman Empire was represented in the East by Antony and in the West by Octavius. Antony became involved with Cleopatra and the eastern Roman army became disorganized and more corrupt.

Antigonus and the Parthians

Antigonus, the youngest son of Aristobulus II, was watching all of this from the other side of the Euphrates. He had found refuge with the Parthians. With their aid, he invaded Judea and lured Hyrcan and Phasael into the camp of the Parthians. Antigonus then cut off Hyrcan's ear, thus preventing him from ever serving as high priest. Phasael committed suicide and the Parthians took Hyrcan with them. Antigonus rode into Jerusalem and assumed the royal title and the high priesthood under the name of Mattathias in 40 BC.

When Antigonus was installed as king, Herod and his family fled to the south where he secured his family in a fortress and then continued on to Egypt to seek help from Antony. However, Antony was in Rome trying to reconcile with Octavius. Herod continued on to Rome where he was warmly received. The Roman Senate proclaimed Herod King of Judea, but he had to win Judea by driving Antigonus out. Rome laid siege on Jerusalem, the slaughter was so great that Herod had to promise large rewards to stop the massacre. Antigonus was captured and executed to avenge the death of Phasael, Herod's brother. In 37 BC, Herod became the unchallenged ruler of Judea.

Herod had forty prominent Sadducees executed and confiscated their property. He used this resource to bribe Roman soldiers and to develop an army of mercenary Jews from the Diaspora. He killed off all remaining members of the Hasmonean family.

Herod totally ruled, and through him, Rome ruled. The Sadducees and the Pharisees had no power. There were many zealots and numerous revolts. One of the more famous rebel leaders was Hezekiah. He was captured and executed by Herod. The Jews demanded that the Sanhedrin bring Herod to trial for the murder of Hezekiah under the Jewish Law; they attempted to do so but the plans were thwarted by Hyrcan II who was, by virtue of his office of high priest, the president of the Sanhedrin. He adjourned the meeting until the next day, and Herod went fuming off to the Roman governor of Syria where he was honored. It was clearly demonstrated that Rome had little regard for "self-rule" in Judea.

Herod was the greatest builder in Jewish history. He expanded the Temple, Masada, the Herodium, Sebaste (Samaria), and the theater in Jerusalem, and built the Port at Caesarea Maritime, to name a few.

The aging Herod the Great called his first son, Antipater II, out of exile to be co-regent. Antipater II plotted to kill his father, but Herod had Antipater II executed. In his will, Herod divided his kingdom between his three sons (Herod Archelaus, Herod Antipater, also known as Herod Antipas, and Philip, the Tetrarch).

Herod Antipas divorced his Nabatean wife, who was the daughter of Aretas IV (the king of all the desert kingdoms), to marry Herodias. She was the wife of his brother Philip. He built Tiberias, beheaded John the Baptist, and questioned and mocked Jesus.

Herod the Great - Family Tree

Herod the Great was married to:
- Doris, a Hellenized Idumean; their son Antipater II (executed 4 BCE)
- Mariamne I, daughter Hasmonean Alexandros (executed 29 BCE)
    Children
    - Alexander (executed 7 BCE)
    - Aristobulus (executed 7 BCE)
    - Salome (daughter)
    - Cypros (daughter)
- Mariamne II, daughter of high Priest Simon
    Children
    - Herod II
- Malthrace, a Samaritan
    Children
    - Herod Archelaus (Ethnarch)
    - Herod Antipas (Antipater III) Tetrarch
    - Olympias (daughter)
- Cleopatra of Jerusalem
    Children
    - Philip the Tetrarch
- Phallas
    Children
    - Phasael
- Phaidra
    Children
    - (daughter) Roxanne
- Elpis
    Children
    - Salome (daughter)
- A cousin (name unknown)
- A niece (name unknown)

The stage is now set in this historical context of Israel at the time of Jesus, and specifically the week of the crucifixion.

In the next chapter, we will take a look at the triumphal entry of Jesus on Palm Sunday.

☙

REFERENCES

Bromiley, G. W. (Ed.). (1979). *The international standard Bible encyclopedia.* Grand Rapids, MI: Wm. B. Eerdmans Publishing Company.

Grayzel, S. (1984). *A history of the Jews from the Babylonian exile to the present 5728-1968.* New York, NY: Meridian.

Whiston, Wm. (1999). *The new complete works of Josephus.* Grand Rapids, MI: Kregel Publications.

CHAPTER TWELVE

The Triumphal Entry

DISCUSSION QUESTION: Who was the crowd waiting for Jesus on Palm Sunday?

Palm Sunday

In 30 AD, the population in Israel was fifty percent pagans and the Jews themselves were divided: the Hellenistic Jews, the Pharisees who were committed to the law and discipline, the Sadducees who were the aristocrats, the Zealots who hated Rome and wanted independence, the Essenes who lived a monastic life, and the Jesus movement. There was high unemployment because Herod's temple was completed and those who worked on it were out of jobs. The Precept, Pontius Pilate, and the religious leaders repeatedly clashed. Jerusalem was crowded with pilgrims. The potential for unrest was great.

The gathering of a crowd on the Mount of Olives would not have gone unnoticed by the religious and political authorities. Who was the crowd that was standing on the Mount of Olives on the Sunday that Christians now refer to as Palm Sunday? They were most probably pilgrims, as the local residents would have been working on the first day of the week. But why were they there? Could it be that they were waiting there in anticipation of Jesus arrival?

It is believed among some scholars that the date of the Messiah's arrival was known because they calculated it from the prophecy in the book of Daniel. If that is the case, then the crowd waiting for Jesus were informed Jews who had studied the scriptures. They knew it was the time for the Messiah to come, and they were prepared to welcome Him.

The surrounding area of Jerusalem and the hillsides would have been covered with camp sites and pilgrim campers. The roads leading into Jerusalem would have been thronged with pilgrims arriving for the feast. Many of these would have known of the blind that received their sight, the lame that could walk, the lepers that were cleansed, the deaf that could hear, the dead that were raised, and the poor that had the gospel preached to them. When John the Baptist sent his disciples to ask Jesus if He was the one that should come, Jesus answered him with this evidence. Many in the crowd would have known of these miracles and would have had the same understanding that John had—Jesus was the long awaited *Messiah* (Mt. 11:5-6). There must have been quite an excitement in the crowd as they waited.

It is doubtful that the religious leaders were among the crowd on the Mount of Olives. They considered Jesus a political rival. The position of high priest had been political since the return from Babylon. Just as Herod had considered the birth of the Messiah to be a threat, the religious leaders also viewed Him as a threat.

The crowd that was there that Sunday had been living under Roman rule for too many years. They longed to regain their independence. They had been oppressed by their religious leaders as well, and they wanted justice, the justice of the Messiah. They were looking for a deliverer. They were waiting for the conquering King Messiah.

"*Tell ye the daughter of Zion, Behold your King comes unto you meek and sitting on a donkey*" (Mt. 21:5).

There were two different perceptions of what exactly was to transpire that day—the divine and the human. Both were clearly illustrated as Jesus entered Jerusalem. He rode in on a donkey. Abram saddled a donkey the morning he offered Isaac as a sacrifice (**Gen. 22:3**). A donkey had been used to speak to the stubborn man Balaam, as recorded in **Numbers 22:21-35**. Tradition has Mary riding on a donkey (although it is doubtful they had a donkey; they most probably walked). But for a king to arrive on a donkey meant only one thing—he was coming in peace not as a conqueror, because a conquering king arrived on a horse.

"*When they heard that Jesus was coming to Jerusalem, they took branches of palm trees, and went forth to meet him*" (**Jn. 12:12-13**).

The crowd had palm branches with them. Palm branches were a symbol of triumph and victory. They had been used when Jehu was anointed king in **2 Kings 9:13**. In **Revelation 7:9**, the multitude that stood before the Lamb had palm branches in their hands. The Maccabees waved palm branches to celebrate independence. The Romans gave palms to the victor in games, and Emperors gave palms to their subjects for military conquest. Palm branches clearly were used to celebrate victory.

Palms did not grow in Jerusalem at the time of Jesus. The nearest palm trees would have been in Jericho, a two-day journey from Jerusalem. That means they came prepared with the palm branches, having cut them in Jericho and carried them to Jerusalem. . . . *and [many people] cried Hosanna: Blessed is the King of Israel that comes in the name of the Lord* (**Jn. 12:13**). In **Psalm 118:26**, we find the same wording, "*blessed is he that comes in the name of the Lord.*"

Hosanna in the Hebrew means *save*, or *save now*. This verse is part of the Hillel. In the Greek New Testament, it becomes an exclamation of praise, but in the Hebrew, it was a *plea for deliverance*. The crowd was clear, they wanted victory, they wanted salvation, but their idea of salvation was to be delivered from Roman oppression.

The crowd and Jesus were experiencing the same physical event at the same time, but with totally different understanding. They wanted Him to deliver them from the enemy of Rome. He came to deliver them from their eternal enemy. They wanted a political solution to bring peace—He came to give eternal peace with God. Their view and hopes were temporal—His was eternal. The triumph of the triumphal entry is victory over our eternal enemy *sin*, not the Romans.

In the days following the triumphal entry, Jesus went on to cleanse the temple. The money-changers referred to in **Matthew 21:12** were tables where coins with Roman inscriptions could be exchanged for temple currency. His authority was challenged by the chief priest and elders, and in response, Jesus used their tradition of asking the questioner a question. The Pharisees tried to trap him with flattery followed by the question of taxes. The Sadducees presented him with the dilemma of the woman whose husbands kept dying, leaving her childless. Throughout the week Jesus continued to teach and minister knowing that His last meal with his disciples was quickly approaching. In the next chapter, we will look at the daily service in the temple at the time of Jesus.

○ℜ

REFERENCES

Isbouts, J. P. (2013). *In the footsteps of Jesus: A chronicle of his life and the origins of Christianity.* Washington, DC: National Geographic.

Maier, P. L. (1997). *In the fullness of time.* Grand Rapids, MI: Kregel Publications.

Ware, T. (1997). *The Orthodox Church.* New York, NY: Penguin Books.

CHAPTER THIRTEEN

Daily Service in the Temple

DISCUSSION QUESTION: How were the Passover lambs slain?

At the first sign of the dawn, a priest would stand in the priest's tower above the Temple Gate and blow the ram's horn. The gates were then opened to allow the crowds to enter. The daily service, with music and the Levites chanting the Psalm, would then begin. Following this, the priests brought the sacrifice. When the sacrifice was completed, the priests faced the crowd with uplifted arms and pronounced the blessing (Ex. 29:38-46).

During the Roman period, after the public sacrifice, the priest made a sacrifice for the safety of the emperor. Pilate's officers actually provided the bullock and two lambs for the emperors' sacrifice. This was an agreement between the Jews and Rome in substitution for the worship of the emperor.

The rest of the day was for private sacrifices. The last sacrifice of the day was for the entire nation, and as the night began to fall, the crowd was dismissed with the priestly blessing and the temple gates were closed.

Preparation for Passover

In antiquity, long before the week of Passover, preparations for the feast would begin. Roads and bridges were repaired to accommodate the estimated two million pilgrims making their way to Jerusalem. Throughout the land, all sepulchers were white washed to protect pilgrims who might accidentally touch one and become unclean.

The command regarding touching a dead body is found in **Numbers 19:11-22**. In these verses, a man who touched a dead body must purify himself on the third day, and on the seventh day, he would be considered clean. If a man did not purify himself, he was said to have defiled the tabernacle of the Lord, and he would be cut off from Israel. The instructions continue to include entering a tent where someone has died, rendering the same uncleanness and need for purification. The rabbis included in this the prohibition of touching the tombs of the dead. So, if a man accidentally touched a tomb or a grave on his way to Jerusalem to celebrate the Passover, he would be rendered unclean and would not be able to participate in the rituals. When Jesus compared the scribes and the Pharisees to whitened sepulchers, this would have been a very clear picture for them.

There was a provision made for a man who became unclean within seven days of the Passover (**Num. 9:6-11**) where they are instructed to keep the Passover in the following month on the fourteenth day. An example of this Second or Minor Passover is found in **2 Chronicles 30:1-5**.

Traditionally, in preparation for the Passover, women who were suspected of adultery were taken to the priests, in accordance with **Numbers 5:11-31**. The priest would then administer the bitter water which was made with the dust of the tabernacle floor, which would cause a curse if the woman had been unfaithful.

Passover also traditionally became the time where Hebrew servants wishing to remain with their masters had their ears pierced as directed in **Exodus 21:1-6**, and it had become the tradition that two weeks before the Passover flocks and herds were tithed in accordance to **Exodus 13:3, 12-13**. So, it is evident that weeks before the Passover throughout the country, the Jews were involved in various preliminary preparations for the week of the feast.

Finally, they would come up to Jerusalem. The pilgrims came from Rome, Greece and from throughout the known world. The Jews were first dispersed by the Babylonian captivity, but not all Jews returned with Ezra and Nehemiah. The majority remained in Babylon. Many Jews had migrated as far away as India. The first Jewish community established there was in Bombay. There were a million Jews living in Alexandria, and untold numbers living throughout the Roman Empire, which basically covered the entire civilized world.

The pilgrims, mostly male, would need to rent housing. The available housing would be taken by the wealthier Jews. Arrangements would be made ahead of time through contacts in Jerusalem. A similar situation continues today for Christian Pilgrims coming to Jerusalem during the Easter Week. Local churches contact the Christians living in Jerusalem to rent rooms for pilgrims. In the time of Jesus, the overflow of pilgrims would camp on the hillsides surrounding Jerusalem as Jesus and His disciples did.

The pilgrims traditionally sang **Psalm 126** as they ascended to Jerusalem:

When the Lord turned again the captivity of Zion,
We were like them that dream.
Then was our mouth filled with laughter,
And our tongue with singing;
Then said they among the heathen,
The Lord hath done great things for them.
The Lord hath done great things for us;
Whereof we are glad.
Turn again our captivity,
O Lord, as the streams in the south.
They that sow in tears shall reap in joy.
He that goes forth and weepeth,
Bearing precious seed,
Shall doubtless come again with rejoicing,

Bringing his sheaves with him

Imagine, with me, that you are living at the time of Jesus on the outskirts of Jerusalem, perhaps in Bethany on the other side of the Mount of Olives. About two weeks before Passover in the late afternoon, you hear the voices of a small group of pilgrims. The breeze carries the sound, but they are not close enough yet for the words to be distinct. But your heart jumps, and you join in the singing, because you know the Psalm. It is the song of the pilgrims. In the following days, there are a few more groups—some arrive earlier in the day so that the voices of the pilgrims are heard sporadically several times throughout the day. Then the week of the feast there is a continual parade of pilgrims making their way to Jerusalem, and the very atmosphere is pregnant with their song!

DURING THE TIME OF JESUS: Ceremonial Cleansing

John 11:55 "... *many went up to Jerusalem before the Passover to purify themselves.* In and around Jerusalem there were ceremonial baths where pilgrims could make themselves ceremonially clean. Ritual purity was required of the Jew before going onto the Temple Mount. These ceremonial baths, in Hebrew, are called Mikvahs. It was required that the water in the baths be running, or living water. This was accomplished through a small drain in the floor of the bath and the continual flow of fresh water entering the bath.

The Mikvahs had two sets of stairs that were divided by a low wall. The bath was entered into by the stairs on the right. The supplicant would walk into the bath until his entire body, including his head, was immersed in the water. This immersion needed to be witnessed by another person. Matthew 3:1-12 is the description of John the Baptist's ministry. This was taking place in the Jordan River, which was qualified as *living water* (i.e. water that is continually moving). John witnessed *those who entered the river*—that is what is meant by the "baptism of John". After the immersion was witnessed in the Mikvah, the supplicant would exit the bath using the stairs on the left because the stairs on the right were used when he was not clean, therefore to walk on them would invalidate his cleansing.

It is interesting to note here that when Jesus was baptized in **Matthew 3:13-17**, He came out of the water and the Spirit of God descended upon Him, and the voice of God proclaimed His pleasure in Him. Jesus' baptism was witnessed by the Holy Spirit and the Father.

Room for the Last Supper

"Now on the first day of Unleavened Bread, when they killed the Passover lamb, His disciples said to Him, "Where do you want us to go and prepare, that you may eat the Passover?" So He sent out two of His disciples and said to them; "Go into the city and a man will meet you carrying a pitcher of water; follow him. And wherever he goes in, say to the master of the house, 'the Teacher says, "Where is the guest room in which I may eat the Passover with my disciples? Then, he will show you a large room, furnished and prepared; there make ready for us" (Mk. 14:12-16).

Jesus and his disciples were camped on the Mount of Olives. It was the day the lamb was to be sacrificed, and in the evening, eaten at the memorial meal. The disciples wanted to make the necessary arrangements so they could eat the meal together. Jesus instructed them to find a man carrying water. It is interesting that a man would be carrying water, since that was the work of women. There was an Essen community living in Jerusalem at that time, it is believed this was a man from that community.

It was common for families, and in this case possibly a community, to rent out rooms which were prepared for the pilgrims to have their Passover meal. The room would have been cleaned and searched for leaven, and the leaven would have been burned by the priest earlier that day. So, it was ceremonially clean to eat the Passover in rooms such as these.

"And his disciples went forth, and came into the city, and found as he had said unto them: and they made ready for the Passover" (Mk. 14:16).

In Jewish homes today, the mother cleans the house from top to bottom, but she will leave a square inch on a wall, usually in the upper corner of the room, untouched. This tradition is intended to remind the observant Jew that nothing can be complete until the temple is rebuilt. This is echoed at Jewish weddings where a glass is broken to remind all that no joy is complete until the temple is rebuilt. After cleaning, the mother carefully hides a portion of leaven for the father and children to find. It is then taken outside and the father burns it reciting a prayer.

Sacrifice at the Temple

In Jerusalem, at the time of Jesus, the priests would burn the leaven in the morning. The leaven that had been searched for by candlelight in each home was brought to the temple to be burned.

The sacrifices would begin at three in the afternoon. The representative pilgrim would take the lamb that would be sacrificed, for everyone in their party, to the temple. So, in the case of Jesus and the disciples, Jesus sent Peter and John (Mt. 22:8) to find the room and to offer the sacrifice.

At the temple the pilgrims were divided into three groups. When a group entered into the temple courtyard, the gates were closed and the ram's horn sounded, then the sacrifice began. Each Jew slaughtered his own lamb. The priests stood in two rows holding basins. The blood was drained into the basin then tossed against the base of the altar. While the offerings were going on, the Levites sang the Hallel (Ps. 113-118).

Each lamb was then skinned, and the fat and kidneys were removed for burning on the altar. Then the offeror wrapped his own lamb in its skin and slung it over his shoulders. He would then roast the lamb in the courtyard of his home. This was repeated three times as each group was admitted into the temple courtyard.

Imagine now, that you have come on this day to offer your sacrifice and that you are part of the second group. On the way up to the temple you would have been part of the crowd—carrying your lamb—you would bump shoulders with others as you stood reverently in line waiting for your group to enter. There would be singing, and the sounds of the lambs baaing. When you arrived, you were placed into the second group. While waiting you hear the ram's horn blast, and then the songs of the Levites begin, almost drowning out the sounds of the lambs being slaughtered. The air fills with the smell of roasted fat, and then the doors open, it is your turn to slaughter your lamb.

On your way home, as you weave your way through the pilgrims' camps that surround Jerusalem, you stop to talk with a few as they roast their lambs. Within the city, every dwelling is full and in every courtyard there is a clay oven with a Passover lamb roasting. The air is heavy with the savory smell of roasting lamb, and the hillsides echo with the Hallel chorus.

Perhaps you wonder why there needed to be the shedding of blood. As you ponder this you begin to recite from the Torah "... *and the Lord commanded the man saying, 'From any tree of the garden you may eat freely; but from the tree of the knowledge of good and evil you shall not eat, for in the day that you eat from it, you shall surely die...* ".(Gen. 2:16-17 NAS) and you remember—it all began in the garden with the rebellion of Adam and Eve.

As you continue to walk, with the weight of the slain lamb heavy on your shoulders, maybe you contemplate what life is. You remember that you are forbidden to eat the blood of an animal (Gen. 9:4) because the life, according to God, is in the blood. It is repeated in the law, "... *for the life of the flesh is in the blood...for it is the life of all flesh, the blood...* (Lev. 17:11-14). Clearly, the Lord has declared that the essence of life is in the blood. If the price for sin is life, then a *blood sacrifice* is required because that is *the essence of life*. Such are your thoughts as you enter the courtyard where you will roast the sacrifice—whose blood was poured on the altar.

The scriptures stating that the *life is in the blood* was confirmed by science in 1616 by William Harvey when he discovered that blood circulation is the key factor in physical life. It carries water and nourishment to every cell (Word of God); it maintains body temperature (Balance); it removes waste material of the body's cells (Cleanses); and it transmits the very *breath of life* by carrying oxygen from the lungs throughout the body to all its cells (Spirit)).

"*In the evening He came with the twelve and as they sat and did eat* . . . ." (Mk. 14:17). The time has arrived for Jesus to have his final meal with His disciples.

☙

REFERENCES

Bromiley, G. W. (Ed.). (1979). *The international standard Bible encyclopedia.* Grand Rapids, MI: Wm. B. Eerdmans Publishing Company.

Edersheim, A. (1976). *The temple: Its ministry and services as they were at the time of Christ.* Grand Rapids, MI: Wm. B. Eerdmans Publishing Company.

Isbouts, J. P. (2013). *In the footsteps of Jesus: A chronicle of his life and the origins of Christianity.* Washington, DC: National Geographic.

Maier, P. L. (1997). *In the fullness of time.* Grand Rapids, MI: Kregel Publications.

Richman, C. (1997). *A house of prayer for all nations: The holy temple of Jerusalem.* Jerusalem, IL: The Temple Institute, Carta.

CHAPTER FOURTEEN

The Passover

DISCUSSION QUESTION: What is the significance of the "blood"?

"And when the hour was come, He sat down, and the twelve apostles with Him..." (Lk. 22:14).

Pesach is the Hebrew word for Passover. In **Exodus 12**, we find the institution of the Passover. *"This month... shall be the beginnings of months: it shall be the first month of the year for you."* (Ex. 12:2).

The Passover was to mark a new beginning for the children of Israel. This month, the month of Abib, was to perpetually begin the Jewish religious calendar—the New Year. The Passover also was the beginning of Jewish national identity and marked the birth of the Jews as a free people. Throughout chapter twelve of Exodus, there are detailed instructions for the observance of the Passover.

We will take a cursory look at this chapter, highlighting the specific instructions given by God for the annual celebration of this feast.

First we note that there was to be a sacrifice offered. The sacrifice was to be *a lamb without blemish* to be taken on the tenth day of the month, but not offered until the fourteenth day of Abib. In other words, the lamb that was to be sacrificed was separated from the flock and observed for four days (it is interesting to note that four is the number symbolic for judgment). In Egypt, the whole congregation of Israel killed their lamb together on the fourteenth of the month and applied the blood of the lamb on the two side posts of the upper door posts. In the temple, the blood was poured on the altar.

As we know, the angel of death passed over the houses with blood applied on the night that all the firstborn of Egypt were killed. This is the historical event that is associated with Passover. The memorial feast was to be kept throughout all their generations.

In **Leviticus 23**, the special feasts days given by the Lord are listed and Passover heads the list. In the fourteenth day of the first month at even is the Lord's Passover (**Lev. 23:5**). Please note that the Passover feast is celebrated for only one day—the fourteenth day of the first month.

Immediately following the Passover, the Feast of Unleavened Bread begins. "... *on the fifteenth day of the same month is the feast of unleavened bread unto the Lord: seven days you must eat unleavened bread* (**Lev. 23:6**). Returning to **Exodus 12:15-19**, they are instructed that "... *there be no leaven found in your houses.* ... The Feast of Unleavened Bread begins on the fifteenth day, the day after the sacrifice of the lamb, and continues for seven days. Unleavened bread was eaten at the Passover meal "... *in the first month on the fourteenth day of the month at even, you shall eat unleavened bread, until the one and twentieth day of the month at even*" (**Ex. 12:18**). In summary, the Passover and the Feast of Unleavened Bread are two separate feasts tied together by the eating of unleavened bread at the Passover meal.

In Hebrew, *leaven* is the word *Hametz*, which is any one of five major grains (wheat, rye, barley, oats, and spelt) that has come into resting contact with water for at least eighteen minutes. Such grain or flour is considered to have begun the leavening process. Hametz also includes anything which has yeast in it.

At this point, it is worth mentioning the symbolism related to these feasts. Egypt, where the children of Israel were in bondage, is symbolic of the "world" where the unredeemed are in bondage to sin. The Passover lamb and the blood on the doorposts are symbolic of the Lord Jesus and His blood that has been shed for us, and that continues to covers us. The unleavened bread is symbolic of freedom from sin, as leaven is symbolic of sin.

In conclusion, the Passover was instituted by God as a memorial feast which commemorates the deliverance of Israel from Egyptian bondage. As such, the Jews were instructed to teach their children the significance of this feast. *And it shall come to pass that when your children shall say unto you, 'what mean you by this service?' That you shall say, 'it is the service of the Lord's Passover, who passed over the houses of the children of Israel in Egypt, when He smote the Egyptians. . . "* (Ex. 12:26-27). The Feast of Unleavened Bread immediately follows the sacrifice of the lamb and is celebrated for seven days—a number which is symbolic of God's perfection, or the number of completion.

The agricultural significance of Passover is that it also marks the harvesting of the barley grain in the land of Israel. The harvesting of the barley was marked by a special offering of the *Omer* (sheaf of barley) on the second day of Passover.

As mentioned in an earlier chapter, the scribes during the Babylonian captivity interpreted the laws found in the Bible and wrote traditional laws in regard to their celebration. The culmination of the traditional laws concerning Passover is found in the Haggadah, which means "the telling". The Haggadah is a book that is used for the order of the Passover Seder (Seder means order). Written into the order of the service is the recounting of the exodus from Egypt and questions for children to ask. This is to ensure that children will ask about the Seder in reference to **Exodus 12:26-27.**

Needed for a Traditional Passover Seder

The following is a list of what is needed for the celebration of a traditional Passover Seder.

▶ **Wine or Non Alcoholic Wine:** This is used throughout the meal because it is a symbol of joy and gladness. There are Four cups because of the *four expressions* used in the Torah in relation to Israel's redemption:
1. I will bring you out
2. I will deliver you
3. I will redeem you
4. I will take you
5. The fifth expression "*I will bring you into the land*" is symbolized by the Fifth Cup which is not drunk. This is called the *Cup of Elijah* who is traditionally the forerunner of the *Messiah*.

▶ **Matzoth** (unleavened bread), which is commanded by the Lord as part of the Passover meal, is given further symbolic meaning as it recalls the haste of their departure from Egypt. It has also come to symbolize, in Jewish tradition, the poor quality of the bread which they ate in Egypt. Since the destruction of the temple, it commemorates the Paschal offering.

▶ **Parsley or celery** is used as a sign of spring, of fruitfulness, and of hope in the future even as it is dipped into the salt water.

▶ **Bitter Herbs** (horseradish or romaine lettuce) symbolize the bitterness they endured during bondage.

▶ **Haroset** (ground apples and walnuts with spices) represents the mortar used by the Israelite's in building the Egyptian cities.

▶ **Dish of salt water** represents the tears of misery shed by the children of Israel.

▶ **One roasted shank bone and one egg** is used to recall the destruction of the Temple and to symbolize the Paschal offering and the festival offering.

▶ **One large wine glass** which is used for Elijah's cup.

▶ **Haggadah** *(the telling)* is a book used for the telling and the order of the service, there should be one for each person present.

At the Time of Jesus

At the time of Jesus, there would have been an order to the service of the Passover meal, which He and His disciples would have followed. It was not as elaborate as the Haggadah in use today. Over the years various Rabbis have added stories and songs to help hold the children's attention. Jesus and His disciples would have recounted the Exodus from Egypt using the various food items in the telling. We know from the gospel accounts this included a hand-washing ceremony and the singing of hymns, both of which are a part of the modern Seder. In addition to the stories and songs that rabbis have added (after the destruction of the temple), the afikomen ritual—which recalls the temple and the sacrifices—was also added.

The following is an abbreviated (without all the stories and songs) version of the Passover Seder as celebrated in Jewish homes today with references to Jesus and His disciples' Passover meal. These accounts are found in:

Matthew 26:17-30
Mark 14:17-26
Luke 22:14-23
John 13:14-20 (washing feet)
John 14:21-30 (dipping sop)

The Order of the Passover Service

The Seder begins when the leader recites the Kiddush—blessing over the wine. This is the first of the four cups of wine used throughout the meal. These cups represent statements the Lord made concerning His deliverance of the children of Israel which are found in **Exodus 6: 6 -7**.

LEADER

*First Cup: The cup of sanctification:

I will bring you out from under the burden of the Egyptians (Ex. 6:6)

*Hold up the first cup of wine and recite the following prayer:

ALL: Blessed art Thou, Eternal our God, Ruler of the universe, Creator of the fruit of the vine. Blessed art Thou, Eternal our God, Ruler of the universe, who chose us from all the peoples and exalted us among all nations, by making us holy with His commandments.

*Drink the first cup of wine.

Jesus was the Leader of the Passover Seder. In Luke 22:17-18 "... *He took the cup and gave thanks and said, "Take this and divide it among yourselves: for I say unto you, I will not drink of the fruit of the vine, until the kingdom of God shall come."*

1. <u>Washing of the hands</u>

Everyone washes their hands in silence. A servant would carry a basin of water around the table for the guests to ceremonially wash their hands.

[Some believe this is when Jesus washed the disciple's feet. In John it is stated that it was after the meal, so it would have been the grace after the meal when He instituted communion John 13:2-17].

2. <u>Eating of the Green Vegetable</u>

LEADER: The leader, master of the house, takes the parsley and dips it into salt water, it is distributed to everyone at the table, and the following blessing is recited by all before they eat it.

ALL: Blessed art Thou, Eternal our God, Ruler of the universe, Creator of the fruit of the earth.

LEADER: As the wine is red in color and represents the blood of the Passover lamb, so also do the greens represent the hyssop which was used to place the blood of the lamb on the doorposts and lintel. The salt water represents the tears shed in Egypt.

[John 13: 21-30 this is when Jesus tells the disciples that one of them who dips with Him will betray Him. The grace of the Lord is so demonstrated in that the other disciples did not know it was Judas, even when He dipped with him, He dipped with everyone.]

3. Break the Middle Matzo and hide half of it for the Afikomen.

LEADER: [The leader, master of the house] breaks the middle matzo in the plate, leaving half of it there. He puts aside the other half until after supper, for the afikomen. The tradition practiced is that the half that has been set aside is hidden for the children to search for later. The child who finds it takes it to the leader, who redeems the half usually with some gift.

[This was not a part of the service at the time of Christ.]

4. Recite the Passover story

ALL: Read together Exodus 12:1-13.

LEADER: Uncover the matzo and lift up the plate for all to see. The recital of the Haggadah begins with the following words:

This is the bread of affliction that our forefathers ate in the land of Egypt. All who are hungry-let them come and eat. All who are needy-let them come and celebrate the Passover with us. Now we are here; next year may we be in the Land of Israel. Now we are slaves: next year may we be free men.

[The plate is put down and the matzo is covered.]

5. Second Cup: The second cup of wine is filled

Cup of Judgment

I will rid you out of their bondage (Exodus 6:6)
The youngest present asks the Four Questions.

The Four Questions

- Why is this night different from all other nights?

LEADER: (Oldest family member replies)
We were slaves to Pharaoh in Egypt and the Lord redeemed us with a mighty hand. If the Holy One, Blessed be His Name, had not taken us out of Egypt, then we would still be Pharaoh's slaves. This is why it is our duty to tell the story of our exodus from Egypt.

Youngest child continues to ask:

- On all other nights, we eat either leavened bread or matzo (unleavened) on this night why only unleavened bread?
- On all other nights, we eat herbs of any kind. On this night why only bitter herbs?
- On all other nights, we do not dip our herbs even once. On this night why do we dip them twice?
- On all other nights, we eat our meals in any manner. On this night why do we sit around the table together in a reclining position.

LEADER: Uncover the matzo and begin the reply
This night is different from all other nights, because on this night we celebrate the going forth of the Jewish people from slavery into freedom.

Why do we eat only Matzo tonight?

When Pharaoh let our forefathers go from Egypt, they were forced to leave in a hurry. They did not have time to wait for the yeast to rise and bake their bread. The sun beat down on the dough and baked it into unleavened bread called matzo.

Why do we eat bitter herbs tonight?

Because our forefathers were slaves in Egypt and their lives were made very bitter.

Why do we dip the herbs twice tonight?

We dip the parsley in salt water because it reminds us of the green of springtime. We dip the bitter herbs in charoesth to remind us that our forefathers were able to endure the bitterness of slavery because it was sweetened with the hope of freedom. Exodus 5

Why do we recline?

Because reclining was the sign of a free man, and since our forefathers were freed on this night we recline at the table.

[It is at this point in modern Seder that the story of the four sons is told, because there are different types of children and therefore the story has to be told in different ways.]

6. <u>Blessing and Reading</u>

LEADER: Blessed be God, who keeps His promise to Israel, blessed be He. For God foretold the end of bondage to Abraham at the Covenant of Sacrifices.

ALL: READ Genesis 15: 12-18

LEADER: Raise the cup of wine and say:

This promise made to our forefathers holds true also for us. For more than once, have they risen against us to destroy us. In every generation they rise against us and seek our destruction. But the Holy One, blessed be He, saves us from their hands.

Put down cup.

7. <u>Reading</u>

ALL: Read Exodus 13:5-22.
Sing Let My People Go (optional)

8. Plagues

Spill a drop of juice for each plague as it is named.

LEADER: These are the ten plagues, which the Most Holy, blessed be His Name, brought on the Egyptians in Egypt.

All recite the plagues together as drop of juice is spilled:

> Blood
> Frogs
> Vermin
> Flies
> Pestilence
> Boils
> Hail
> Locusts
> Darkness
> Slaying of the first-born

9. Reading-Singing

ALL: Read Exodus 12:1-14
ALL: Sing Dayenu

The men can all read the verses together and everyone sing the chorus of Dayenu.

Men: If He had merely rescued us from Egypt, but had not punished the Egyptians.

DAYENU 5xs

Men: If He had merely punished the Egyptians, but had not destroyed their gods.

DAYENU 5xs

Men: If He had merely destroyed their gods, but had not slain their first born.

DAYENU 5xs

Men: If He had merely slain their first born, but had not given us their property.

DAYENU 5xs

Men: If He had merely given us their property but had not parted the sea for us.

DAYENU 5xs

Men: If He had merely parted the sea for us, but had not brought us through on dry ground [font changes again].

DAYENU 5xs

Men: If He had merely brought us through on dry ground, but had not drown our oppressors.

DAYENU 5xs

Men: If He had merely drowned our oppressors, but had not supplied us in the desert for forty years.

DAYNEU 5xs

Men: If He had merely supplied us in the desert for forty years, but had not fed us with manna.

DAYENU 5xs

Men: If He had merely fed us with manna, but had not given us the Sabbath.

DAYENU 5xs

Men: If He had merely given us the Sabbath, but had not brought us to Mount Sinai.

DAYENU 5xs

Men: If He had merely brought us to Mount Sinai, but had not given us the Torah.

DAYENU 5xs

Men: If He had merely given us the Torah, but had not brought us to the land of Israel.

DAYENU 5xs

Men: If He had merely brought us to the land of Israel, but had not built us the Temple.

DAYENU 5xs and repeat another 5xs

10. Three Symbols

LEADER: Rabbi Gamliel used to say: Whoever does not explain the following three symbols at the Seder on Passover has not fulfilled his duty:

> The Passover Offering Paschal
> The Matzo
> The Bitter Herbs

LEADER: Takes hold of the shank bone, shows it to the company, and recites: The *Paschal Lamb* that our forefathers ate in Temple times—*for what reason*?

Because the Holy One, blessed be His Name, spared the houses of our ancestors in Egypt, as it is written in the Bible:

"*. . . You shall declare, this is the Passover offering unto the Lord who passed over the house of the children of Israel when He struck Egypt and spared our houses. Then the people bowed in worship.*"

LEADER: Point to the *Matzo*.

This matzo which we eat, what is the reason for it?

It is because there was not time for the dough of our ancestors in Egypt to become leavened when the Lord God redeemed them, as is told in the Bible: And the dough which they had brought out from Egypt they baked into cakes of unleavened bread because they were thrust out of Egypt and they could not tarry.

LEADER: Point to the *bitter herbs*.

These bitter herbs which we eat-what is their meaning?

They are eaten to recall that the Egyptians embittered the lives of our forefathers in Egypt. As it is written,". . . *they embittered their lives with hard labor: with mortar and bricks, with every kind of work in the fields; all the works which they made them do was rigorous.*"

In every generation one must look upon himself as if he personally had come out from Egypt, as the Bible says: And thou shalt tell thy son on that day, saying, it is because of that which the Lord God did to me when I went forth from Egypt. For it was not alone our forefathers were redeemed, the Lord God redeemed us with them.

LEADER: Raise the cup of wine.

Therefore, it is our duty to thank and praise in song and prayer, to glorify and extol Him Who performed all these wonders for our forefathers and for us. He brought us out from slavery to freedom, from anguish to joy, from sorrow to festivity, from darkness to great light. Let us therefore sing before Him a new song. Praise the Eternal.

LEADER: Put down the cup of wine.

11. <u>Reading</u>

ALL: Read Psalms 113-114

Worship songs may be substituted here

LEADER: Raise the cup of wine and say (this is still the second cup).

In truth we can say Praise the Lord for the great redemption which He has wrought on our behalf; redemption with a high cost; in Egypt the death of the firstborn.

Redemption from sin, the death of God's Son (Jn. 3:16).

12. <u>Blessing for second cup:</u>

ALL: Blessed art thou Oh Lord our God, Ruler of the universe, Creator of the fruit of the vine.

[Drink the Second Cup]

13. <u>Washing Hands</u>

[Everyone washes their hands; do not speak until after the blessing is recited]

ALL: recite the following blessing as the hands are cleansed.

Praised art Thou O Lord our God, Ruler of the universe, Who has sanctified us by Thy commandments and commanded us concerning the washing of the hands.

14. Eating of the Matzo

LEADER: The upper matzo is broken and distributed. The following two blessing are recited in unison before eating.

Praised art Thou, O Lord our God, Ruler of the universe who brings forth bread from the earth.

Praised art Thou, O Lord our God, Ruler of the universe, Who has sanctified us by Thy commandments, and has commanded us to eat matzo.

[Everyone now eat the matzo.]

15. Bitter Herb

All: Recite the following blessing.

Praised art Thou, O Lord our God, Ruler of the universe, who has sanctified us by Thy commandments, and has commanded us to eat the bitter herb.

[Each person dips the bitter herbs into the charoesth and layers it with matzo as a reminder of the Temple.]

16. Bottom Matzo

LEADER: The bottom matzo on the plate is broken and distributed. Horseradish, charoesth, and the matzo are eaten together, after the leader explains:

[Explanation]:

While the Temple yet stood Hillel (great Rabbi) introduced a custom of his own into the Seder services: he would put together a piece of the Paschal offering, a piece of matzo and a piece of the bitter herb, and eat the three together, in accordance with the verse in the Scripture: They shall eat it upon unleavened bread and bitter herbs.

Note: Today, this is done in remembrance of the Temple.

17. Eat the Passover Meal

18. After the Meal: Afikomen

The afikomen is searched for by the children, when found it is redeemed with a small gift by the master of the house.

Everyone then eats from the afikomen in remembrance of the lambs that were slain when the Temple stood.

Jesus Institutes Communion

It was at this point the afikomen ritual, which was not a part of the Seder at the time of Jesus, because the temple was still standing and sacrifices were still being offered, that Jesus instituted what we know as communion. He knew he would soon be crucified, and that in the near future, the Temple would be destroyed. He also knew that the traditional Jews (those who would not accept Him as the Messiah) would obviously not accept Him as the ultimate sacrifice. Looking into the future, Jesus knew that those Jews would add a part in their Seder to remember the Temple that once stood and the sacrifices that were made.

Jesus, knowing all this, instituted a new part to the Passover Seder for those Jews who did believe on Him, and He instructed them, *"This do in remembrance of me."* (Lk. 22:19). He was basically telling them, that when others do the afikomen ritual in remembrance of the Temple that once stood and the lambs that were once offered, you do this in remembrance of me. Why, because *". . . this cup is the New Testament in my blood which is shed for you"* (Lk. 22:20).

It is important for us to understand the significance of His blood. You remember that, because of rebellion, a blood sacrifice was required for man to have a relationship with God. *Life* was the cost for rebellion *". . . for in the day that you eat thereof you shall surely die. . . "* (Gen. 2:17). We also know that the life is in the blood (Gen. 9:4), therefore a blood sacrifice was needed for man. The blood of Jesus was the ultimate sacrifice for man. What was special about His blood?

"Now the birth of Jesus Christ was as follows, when His mother Mary had been betrothed to Joseph, before they came

together she was found to be with child by the Holy Spirit." (**Mt. 1:18 NAS**)

The blood of an unborn baby is produced within the body of the fetus itself after the introduction of the male sperm. An unfertilized egg can never develop blood. Only after the male element has entered the ovum does blood develop. The male element gives life. The Holy Spirit fertilized the egg within Mary's womb in a mysterious way, and the blood that flowed through Jesus Christ's veins was the very blood of God—perfect and suitable for sacrifice. God, Himself, provided the blood sacrifice for humanity (**Gen. 22:8**).

"*Behold the Lamb of God, who takes away the sin of the world*" (**Jn. 1:29**).

"*... He appeared to put away sin by the sacrifice of Himself*" (**Heb. 9:26**).

"*Who was delivered for our offences, and was raised again for our justification*" (**Rom. 4:25**).

One must have an understanding of the significance of the blood of Jesus to understand and appreciate Jesus as the Lamb of God, and the declaration that Jesus made to His disciples at their last Passover Seder. "*... And He took the cup, and gave thanks, and gave it to them saying, 'Drink all of it, for this is my blood of the New Testament, which is shed for many for the remission of sins'*" (**Mt. 26:27-28**).

19. Grace after the meal

LEADER: Let us say grace.

ALL: Let us praise Him of whose bounty we have partaken, from this time forth and forever more.

LEADER: Praised art Thou, O Lord our God, Ruler of the universe, who sustains the world with goodness, and with infinite mercy. Thou gives good unto every creature, for Thy mercy endures forever.

ALL: Through Thy great goodness, food has not failed us. May it never fail us at any time, for the sake of Thy great name.

ALL IN UNISON: O Lord our God, sustain and protect us. Grant us to bear our burdens. Let us not become dependent upon men, but let us rather trust Thy hand, which is ever open and gracious, so that we may never be put to shame.

LEADER: Our God, and God of our fathers, be Thou ever mindful of us,

As Thou has been of our fathers. Grant us grace, mercy, life and peace on this Feast of Unleavened Bread.

ALL: Amen

LEADER: Remember us this day in kindness.

ALL: Amen

LEADER: Visit us this day with blessing.

ALL: Amen

LEADER: Preserve us this day for life.

ALL: Amen

LEADER: O give thanks unto the Lord, for He is good, for His mercy endures forever.

ALL: Thou open Thy hand and satisfy every living thing with favor.

LEADER: The Lord will give strength unto His people; the Lord will bless His people with peace.

ALL: Amen

20. <u>Cups are filled for the third time.</u>

Third Cup: Cup of Redemption

I will redeem you with an outstretched arm.(Ex. 6:6)

ALL: Praised art Thou, O Lord our God, King of the universe, Creator of the fruit of the vine.

LEADER: Luke 22:20 | Matthew 26:27-29 | Mark 14:23-25 [Drink the third cup of wine.]

Elijah the Prophet

The door is opened and the fourth and last cup is filled by the LEADER; the Cup of Elijah the Prophet, is set on the table and filled.

ALL: rise as if to greet him. (Elijah, in Jewish tradition, is the long expected messenger of the final redemption of mankind from all oppression.)

ALL: *"Bring judgment upon the nations and kingdoms who do not call upon Your name."*

LEADER: There are items on the Seder plate which have not been touched.

The Roasted Egg; speaks of the sacrifice which can no longer be made because the Temple was destroyed.

The Shank bone is untouched because lambs are no longer sacrificed.

21. Fourth Cup

LEADER: Fill the Fourth Cup.

We come to the fourth and last drinking cup. This cup represents the fourth: *"I will take you to me for a people"* (Ex. 6:7).

[Drink the fourth and final cup.]

ALL: Singing of songs. (Worship Songs) (Mt. 26:30, and Mk. 14:26)

And when they had sung hymns they went out to the Mount of Olives.

22. Conclusion of the Seder

LEADER: Ended is the Passover Seder according to custom, statute, and law.

ALL:

> As we were worthy to celebrate it this year,
> So may we perform it in future years.
> O Pure One in heaven above,
> Restore the congregation of Israel in Your love.
> Speedily lead your redeemed people
> To Zion in joy.
> Sing: La Shanna Ha Ba

ALL: NEXT YEAR IN JERUSALEM.

REFERENCES

Bromiley, G. W. (Ed.) ( ) .*The international standard Bible encyclopedia*. Grand Rapids, MI. Wm. B. Eerdmans Publishing Company.

Donin, H. H. (1972). *To be a Jew*. New York, NY: Basic Books.

Edersheim, A. (1976). *The temple: Its ministry and services as they were at the time of Christ*. Grand Rapids, MI: Wm. B. Eerdmans Publishing.

Maier, P. L. (1997). *In the fullness of time*. Grand Rapids, MI: Kregel Publications.

CHAPTER FIFTEEN

PILATE

DISCUSSION QUESTION: Would it have been possible for Pilate to release Jesus?

First Citizens of Rome

Rome was governed by the Principate Princeps (first citizens) of the Empire. The Princep (or Emperor) at the time of Pilate was Tiberius. Tiberius stayed on Capri throughout most of his reign, leaving Lucius Aelius Sejanus, the Praetorian Prefect (commander of the Praetorian Troops) in charge of most administrative affairs.

Pontius Pilate

Pontius Pilate was born a few years before Jesus in Italy or possibly Rome. He was the descendant of the mountain men from Samnium which was located south of Rome. The Samniums fought Rome for many years. In 321 BC, Gavius Pontius, an ancestor of Pilate, humiliated the Roman army at a high mountain pass called the Caudine Forks. He took away their weapons, made them strip to their tunics, and drove them home under a triumphal yoke of three spears lashed together. However in 290 BC, Rome defeated the Samniums who eventually became Roman citizens. Julius Caesar recruited Samnite men for their valor. They became *equites illustriores* (equestrians), then special administrators, prefects, and private imperial trouble-shooters.

Pontus Pilate was from the tribe of Pontii as indicated by the name *Pontius*. The Pontii were a tribe of Samnite royalty. Pilatus, according to Wroe, means skilled with the *javelin*. The *pilum* (javelin) was a five foot wooden shaft and two feet of tapered iron, the bottom half of which was left soft and untempered. When the point of the javelin lodged in a shield the shaft would bend and hang making it impossible to throw back. William Malicoat attributes this description to the name Pontius, rather than Pilate. Malicoat reports that *pileatus* in Latin means *wearing the pileus*—the cap or badge of a freedman. Pilate was probably no more than second generation removed from a former slave.

When Pilate became of age, he would have prepared for public service, which usually meant a commission in the army as a junior officer, for which he would need a recommendation. He would then serve somewhere in the empire for several years before returning to Rome. The wars in which Pilate fought would have been viewed by him as wars waged for the furthering of civilization. His tours of duty would have earned him entrance into the *eques* or, better known to us, as the *equestrian class*.

It is possible that Pilate, upon his return to Rome, became a member of the Praetorian Guard, the personal bodyguards of the emperor. Lucius Aelius Sejanus was the commander of the Praetorian Guard from 23—31 AD, and it is believed by some scholars that Pilate's appointment as Precept of Judea was due to Sejanus recommendation.

In 26 AD, Pilate, accompanied by his wife, Claudia Procula, took up his posting as prefect-governor of Judea. Pilate was at least thirty years old at this time. This was the minimum age requirement for Roman governors. Claudia Procula, from the clan of Proculi, was of imperial bloodline and the fact that she accompanied her husband to his overseas posting is believed to be an indicator of a great love between husband and wife.

Wives were seen as a security risk and did not go with their husbands. Additionally, life in remote provinces of the empire was difficult. Not only did Claudia Procula go with Pilate to Judea, she also accompanied him on his trips to Jerusalem. This was a tiresome trip from Caesarea, and furthermore, Jerusalem was decidedly unsafe.

Pilate commanded an army of four-thousand men; only the senior officers were Romans. The troops were Idumeans, Samarians, and Syrians. It does not escape ones' attention that Pilate's forces were historical enemies of the Jews.

The role of the Roman Prefect in Judea was to secure tax revenues, establish trade and keep the peace—the latter proving to be the greatest challenge for Pilate. In Judaea, Pilate was the chief soldier, chief magistrate, and the head of the judicial system. The Jews, however, dealt with most of their own civil and criminal issues through their councils. Judea was a small province so Pilate did not have the large staff that the governors of the larger provinces had.

Pilate had no *lictors*—two men who walked in front of the magistrate carrying the *fasces* (a bundle of elm rods bound with an ax) as a symbol of penal authority. Neither did he have a *questor*—one who did the background questioning of a defendant at a magisterial hearing.

Pilate took up his posting in Judea in 26 AD. Although he was required by Rome to keep detailed records, and he most certainly would have done so, all the records which Pilate kept have disappeared. Tacitus probably would have mentioned him, but the two chapters that cover 30—31 AD have also disappeared. There is minimal mention of him by Josephus, and Philo of Alexandria. The most detailed mention of Pilate in historical records is in the New Testament.

In 1961, in Caesarea, a large block was found, and the inscription in Latin read: Pontius Pilate of Judaea has given this Tiberieum to the citizens of Caesarea. This is believed to have been placed in a building that was honoring Tiberius. Coins that Pilate minted have also been found. They were tiny, only

¾ of an inch across and weighing about 2 grams. The coins that have survived are made of bronze and have images of objects used in Roman religious practices. These are the only surviving artifacts found that related to Pilate.

During most of Pilate's time as Prefect of Judea, Tiberius was executing his enemies, real or imagined. It is said that from the slightest word of an informer, one's execution could be ordered. Pilate would have been receiving reports of this, and no doubt was interested in impressing Tiberius with his loyalty to him. Especially after Sejanus, who is believed to have recommended Pilate to Tiberius for the position as Prefect, fell from grace. It seems that no one at this time could trust that they were in favor with the Emperor.

In addition to the intrigue of Rome, there was the political intrigue in Israel and the surrounding countries. In Israel, Agrippa was moving to advance his own claims to be ruler of Judea. Lucius Seius Strabo, in Egypt, had been the commander of the Praetorian Guard before his appointment as governor of Egypt, and as such, would have a solid relationship with Tiberius. Aelius Lamia, who was not trusted, was legate of Syria. Pomponius Flaccus, the governor, had been called back to Rome and was there for five years during Pilate's 10 year tenure.

Pilate was surrounded by ambitious politicians. Agrippa actually wrote to Tiberius to complain that Pilate was inflexible and stubborn. Pilate's sponsor, Sejanus, had fallen out of favor with the Emperor, who was on a tirade executing perceived enemies. Among those that Tiberius disliked and therefore did not fully trust, were the Samnites, which was Pilate's heritage. Added to this was the fact that Pilate had not been given an appointment for a pre-determined length of time—he was on probation. Given all these circumstances, one can easily understand Pilate's continued efforts to please Tiberius. Unfortunately, those efforts offended the Jews.

The Standards

Throughout the Roman Empire, the Jews were the only people who did not worship the Roman emperors. Jerusalem was the only city in the empire where the citizens did not bow in public to worship the image of the Emperor. There were images of the Emperor throughout the entire Roman world and his image was carried on sacred standards of the army which were carried by every unit. The troops were in the habit of dismantling the images attached to the standards before they entered Jerusalem, the holy city of the Jews.

The image attached to the standards was a gold medallion about six inches across enclosed in a border engraved like a triumphal wreath bound with ribbons. This was attached to the standard a foot from the top and could be easily removed. The Augustan Cohort of the Sebastians from Sebaste (also known as Samaria) had distinguished themselves by putting down a zealot revolt and were rewarded by receiving the name of Augustan Cohort and a special medallion with the image of the emperor on their standards. When it came time for Pilate to rotate his troops, he sent the Augustan Cohort, with their iconic standards, to Jerusalem. They entered the city under the cover of darkness and placed the standards on the walls of the Antonia Fortress, which was occupied by the Roman army. This rotation of the Augustan Cohort and the planting of Roman standards in a Roman occupied place at the start of Pilate's term were intended to show the Jews who was in charge.

The Jews considered the standards to be blasphemous. They demanded that Pilate remove them. Pilate refused. To protest, the Jews walked to Caesarea, some with their feet bound in rags, and gathered in the street outside of Pilate's palace. They stood praying with their ritual swaying—demanding that Pilate remove the standards. On the sixth day, Pilate forced a confrontation. His soldiers had their swords drawn but the Jews, unafraid of death, bared their necks to the soldiers. Pilate relented and removed the standards. This was a strategic error. Pilate's humility delighted the Jews, so much so, that they added a new feast day: the 3rd of Kislev to commemorate the day the standards were removed.

It is interesting to note that these standards were removed without requesting permission from the emperor. This indicates that the placing of the standards in Jerusalem was Pilate's own idea, and that he had not consulted Tiberius.

The Aqueduct

The second conflict with the Jews occurred when Pilate decided to build a much needed aqueduct for Jerusalem. He met with the high priest and the Sanhedrin to propose that temple funds be used to build an aqueduct to bring much needed water to Jerusalem. This was agreed upon. A forty mile aqueduct that was lined with lead and lime mortar was built using *corban* (temple funds). The aqueduct was in use when the general Jewish population discovered that temple funds were used to finance the project. The Jewish public demanded that Pilate replace the funds. Pilate refused. The Jews demonstrated, shouting that Pilate had touched holy money and defiled the temple. This time, Pilate was prepared for their protests and had his soldiers, dressed as Jews, carrying daggers among the crowd. When Pilate gave the signal, his legionnaires attacked the unarmed Jews and many were killed (Lk. 13:1). Again, this was seen as a political mistake especially because, at this time, Tiberius was extending favor to the Jews.

Meanwhile, Rome was involved in its own intrigue. Tiberius remained on Capri. Agrippina (Nero's mother) continued her manipulation and competition for power. Sejanus, who had fallen from favor, was executed. All those who supported Sejanus were seen as enemies of the state and many were executed. Pilate's position as Prefect of Judea and Samaria was believed to be a direct result of Sejanus' position and his relationship with Tiberius. Pilate was vulnerable and under a great deal of pressure to demonstrate he was a capable and loyal servant of Rome.

The Aspiedeion

Unbeknownst to Pilate, Tiberius had forbidden all proposals of honor, when he had *aspiedeion* shields made. The name, *aspiedeion*, meant that it was made and dedicated in thanks for services rendered. Pilate had the *aspiedeion* shields made. They were coated in gold and dedicated in honor of Tiberius. Shields like this were usually hung in public buildings or in a temple of a god. Pilate had the shields hung in Herod's palace in Jerusalem, on the walls in his own apartment.

Once again, the Jews objected and wanted the shields removed. Pilate refused. To Pilate, the shields were holy, they had been dedicated, and he could not take them down. Herod Antipas and Philip the Tetrarch pleaded with Pilate to take the shields down. They reportedly told him that he did not honor the emperor by dishonoring ancient laws. Pilate was adamant, the shields would remain. Antipas and Philip left and wrote a letter to Tiberius. The Emperor, in response, wrote a scathing letter to Pilate demanding that he take the shields down and move them to Caesarea.

Pilate, in retaliation, withdrew from the Sanhedrin the right of execution for capital crimes. The Sanhedrin could try the cases, but sentencing and execution would be carried out by the Prefect of Judea. *Jus gladii* is Latin for Supreme Jurisdiction. It literally means *right to the sword*. This was the right to absolve from or condemn a man to death. This authority was now in the hands of Pilate.

Inquisitorial System

Roman government was an Inquisitorial system which involved three phases in the pursuit of justice. The court may investigate, gather facts and ask questions: 1) Accusatio; 2) Interrogatio; 3) Excusatio.

Pilate in Jerusalem

Pilate traveled to Jerusalem with his wife for the Passover Feast. The city was crowded with pilgrims making the tense situation with the Jews all the more volatile. On this particular year there was a new threat—a man named Jesus—whom some Jews claimed to be the Messiah, and others were determined to rid Israel of him. Pilate, like all political leaders, had his spies throughout the land, and they had told him about Jesus. He did not seem to be a threat, but the religious leaders' hatred of Him could cause problems. No doubt all of this was on Pilate's mind as the sounds of lambs bleating and the trumpets blasting filled the city. He would be happy to return to Caesarea, a Roman city that was civilized and quiet on the sea. Pilate, while in Jerusalem, would have stayed at either the Palace, which was on the Western Hill and provided a view of the Temple Mount, or at the Antonian Tower which housed the army. Since his wife had accompanied him, Pilate probably stayed at the palace. The Praetorian was considered to be wherever the Prefect was.

The Trial and Crucifixion

"When morning was come, all the chief priests and elders of the people took counsel against Jesus to put him to death; and when they had bound him, they led him away, and delivered him to Pontius Pilate... "
(Mt. 27:1-20).

According to the Gospel of Nicodemus 1:1, among those who took Jesus to Pilate were Ananias, Caiaphas, Datum, Gamaliel (Paul's mentor), Judas, Levi, Naphthalim, Alexander, Cyrus, and many others.

Pilate was only required to confirm the verdict of the Sanhedrin, but he chose to hear the case. In effect, he reopened the case when he requested a formal bill of indictment. The charges brought against Jesus were: subverting the nation, forbidding payment of tribute money to Tiberius, and claiming that He is Messiah, a king. This claim was construed as *maiestas* which was high treason (**Lk. 23:2**).

Pilate's first line of questioning was in regard to the maiestas charge. He asked, *"Are you the King of the Jews?"* In the Gospel of John, there is a much more detailed account of the trial of Jesus. In **John 18:34**, Jesus responds to Pilate's question by asking a question. Basically Jesus asks, *"Are you saying this because it is a question you have, or is it because of the charge from the religious leaders?"*

In **Luke 23:5** after Pilates' attempt to release Jesus, the Jews accuse Him of "*. . . teaching throughout all Jewry beginning from the Galilee to this place."* When Pilate heard that Jesus was from the Galilee, he sent Him to Herod in an attempt to pass the problem on. [Note: This was Herod Antipas the tetrarch ruler of Galilee (**Lk. 3:1**).]

> *". . . when Herod saw Jesus, he was exceedingly glad: for he was desirous to see Him for a long season, because he heard many things of Him; and he hoped to have seen some miracle. . . "*

Herod questioned Jesus in front of the religious leaders who had brought him, but Jesus was silent. Then "*. . . Herod and his men of war . . . mocked him, and arrayed Him in a gorgeous robe, and sent Him again to Pilate. . .* " (**Lk. 23:8-12**).

Herod was an Idumean (an Edomite). The Edomites were the enemies of the Jews from the time they came up out of Egypt. In the book of Obadiah (which is a prophecy against Edom), the Lord states that they will be cut off forever because of their violence against Israel (referred to as "your brother Jacob"). The prophecy continues to list the offences against Israel. And here is Jesus being questioned and mocked by an Edomite.

Later on in the trial, Jesus refers to the "truth" and Pilate asks, "What is truth?" Behind Pilate's question lay the philosophical debates of the great philosophers. Pilate made repeated attempts to release Jesus, but the Jews accused him of being no friend of Caesars' in **John 19:12**. This is quite possibly a reference to a ring that Pilate had received from Tiberius. Engraved on the ring was **amicus Caesaris** which, translated, means "a friend of Caesars". The insinuation was that, while you are wearing the ring, you are in reality no friend of Caesars if you let this man go.

On every cross a *Titulus* was nailed. This was the crime the crucified was guilty of. Pilate had written on the cross of Jesus: Jesus of Nazareth, the King of the Jews. This gave Pilate a solid reason for the crucifixion. Jesus, the King, did not reign, but was crucified by the Jews because He prophesied the destruction of the city and the devastation of the Temple (Barrett, The New Testament Background: Selected Documents p.207 Tacitus).

- Tacitus, a Roman Historian in his Annals of Imperial Rome, refers to the "originator" of Christianity: "Christ" has been executed...
- **Stated Basis of Sentence**: Constructive treason, implied maiestas;
- **Secondary Basis of Sentence**: Endorsement of Sanhedrin's conviction of Jesus on a capital religious offense;
- **Appeal**: None. The convicted is not a Roman citizen."

The crucifixion of Jesus took place on April 3, 33 AD in the 19th year of Tiberius' reign according to Eusebius and other historical sources.

One final note from **Luke 23:44** ... *and it was about the sixth hour, and there was darkness over all the earth until the ninth hour.*" The eclipse mentioned in this verse occurred on April 3, 33 AD. It was recorded that the darkness was visible in Rome, Athens, and other Mediterranean cities (ref. Tertullian Apologeticus).

Pilate served as Prefect of Judea for ten years. He arrived in 26 AD which means that he remained in Israel for three years after the crucifixion of Jesus. Pilate departed from Israel in late December 36 AD—because he had been dismissed. Pilate had always been on probation and was finally sent home by the governor of Syria. They usually change officers in July.

There have been traditional stories in regard to what happened to Pilate. A very popular one is that he committed suicide. However, there was not a tradition of Pilate's suicide in the 2nd and 3rd centuries; this story developed as part of church tradition much later. There is no evidence of this.

During Tiberius's reign, the Christian name went out into the entire world.

REFERENCES

Bromiley, G. W. (Ed.). (1979). *The international standard Bible encyclopedia.* Grand Rapids, MI: Wm. B. Eerdmans Publishing Company.

Maier, P. L. (1968). *Pontius Pilate.* Garden City, NY: Doubleday & Company, Inc.

Malicoat, William. (2013). *Pontius Pilate and the Crucifixion of Christ.* e-PUB: ISBN 978-1-908994-60-8.

Mercado, Norbert L. (2013). *The Roman Governor of Judaea (In the shadow of the Roman Empire) [Book III].* ASIN: B00CCQU7IA. Kindle Edition.

Tacitus, Cornelius. *The annals of Imperial Rome.* Stilwell. A Digireads.com Book. (2005). (Translated by Alfred John Church and William Jackson Brodribb).

Wroe, Ann. (1999). *Pontius Pilate.* New York, NY: Random House.

CHAPTER SIXTEEN

OLD TESTAMENT FEASTS

DISCUSSION QUESTION: What are the only holidays given by God?

DAY OF REST

"Thus the heaven and the earth were finished, and all the host of them. And on the seventh day God ended His work which He had made; and He rested on the seventh day, and sanctified it: because that in it He had rested from all His work which God created and made" (Gen. 2:1-3).

The seventh day of rest is the first holy day given by God. He set the example in that He rested. Does God need rest? I hardly think so, but the man that God created would need rest, and the Creator provided for that rest. God is not a slave driver. He does not drive man until he collapses. He wants man to take the rest he needs.

In Jewish thought, one of the two themes for the Sabbath is a memorial to creation. The reference for this is in **Exodus 20:11,** *"For in six days the Lord made heaven and earth, the sea, and all that is in them, and rested the seventh day: Wherefore the Lord blessed the Sabbath day and hallowed it."* Then in **Exodus 31:17,** the Lord states, *"It is a sign between me and the children of Israel forever..."* When the observant Jew keeps the Sabbath day of rest, he is doing so remembering that *God is* *the Creator of the Universe* and that, in keeping this holy day, he is reminded that it is a sign of a relationship with the Creator.

The second theme for the Sabbath is found in **Deuteronomy 5:15**. The verse follows the detailed command and instructions for the day of rest. "*...Remember that you were a servant in the land of Egypt, and that the Lord your God brought you out through a mighty outstretched hand: therefore the Lord your God commanded you to keep the Sabbath day.*" In the preceding verses of this passage, the Lord instructs that not only were the children of Israel to keep the Sabbath, but it was to be kept by all in their household, all of their servants, and all of their work animals. Rabbinical thought on this is that the second theme of Sabbath is a memorial to the Exodus from Egypt and thus a weekly protest against slavery.

We find the commands for the observance of the Sabbath in **Exodus 35:2-3**, "*... whosoever does work therein (Sabbath) shall be put to death. You shall kindle no fire throughout your habitations upon the Sabbath day.*" The observance of the Sabbath day as commanded by the Lord involved the cessation of all work and not building a fire. The building of a fire in antiquity required work, and it was possible to "bank" a fire so that there were always live coals that wood could be added to.

It is obvious that the Lord wanted this to be a complete day of rest for everyone, including servants. A day separated from the rest of the week-days that were full of activity—a day when everything and everyone stopped and remembered God who had created the heavens and the earth.

As has been discussed in previous chapters, the scribes of antiquity, and later the rabbis, took it upon themselves to interpret the Law of Moses found in the Torah with additional laws relating how the law applied to daily life. These additional laws are known as the "Fence around the Law". The Fence is intended to prevent any sincere practicing Jew from inadvertently breaking the law. The unspoken thought behind this is that if one does not break the Law one can obtain perfection. Following are some examples of this fence.

To insure that an observant Jew never built a fire on the Sabbath, by traditional law, they are not permitted to turn on electrical lights, nor drive cars, smoke, watch TV, or play video games on the Sabbath. To ensure no work was done there exists hundreds of detailed lists of what constitutes work. We will look at one—the Sabbath's Day Journey—which is a distance of 3,000 feet from one's home. To insure this law is kept, a string was attached to the home and measured out to 3,000 feet.

It is interesting to note that there are orthodox Jews in Israel who believe that if the nation of Israel were to rid the land of all Gentiles and keep all the laws of the Sabbath for one Sabbath day that the Messiah would come. They live in a neighborhood named Mea Shearim, and if you happen to drive a car into their neighborhood on the Sabbath, they will stone you.

Traditional Observances for Shabbath

Lighting the Candles

The Lighting of Shabbath Candles ushers in Shabbath. This is done before sundown on Friday. The Biblical day begins and ends at sundown. In times of antiquity, a ram's horn was blown about 20 minutes before sunset to warn everyone to complete all tasks. At sundown the horn blew again to signal that the Shabbath had begun. In Jerusalem today a type of siren is used for this warning.

The mother of the house lights the Sabbath candles and pronounces the blessing. The candles are placed in a safe place to be able to burn down, because one is not permitted to blow out the Shabbath Candles.

Blessing

Blessed art Thou, Adonai, O king of the universe who has given us the commandment to light the candles of Shabbath.

The day of rest now begins. The women of the house are very tired and ready to rest because they have spent the day preparing for the Shabbath. They had to clean the house, prepare special food for the next 24 hours, and they are ready to rest!

Synagogue

The men, and those women choosing to do so, go to the synagogue to read the Torah and the Prophets together and to pray. This is called the Tenach. When the men return to the house, they greet the women with the greeting of the Sabbath: *Shabbath Shalome.*

Washing of the Hands

Following the greeting all the family members and guests wash their hands. This is done because of the verses in **Psalm 24:3-4** *"Who shall ascend into the hill of the Lord? Or "who may stand in His holy place?"*

Kiddush

After the hands are washed, everyone stands around the table. The father is at the head, and the mother to his right. Everyone becomes silent, and then the father recites the blessing over the wine, the *Kiddush*. The father then takes a sip of the wine and passes it to the mother, who sips and passes it on. The wine goes around the table to each person to sip. There is no talking during this time. After everyone has sipped the wine and the cup has returned to the father, everyone but the father is seated.

Blessing over the Challah

The father now uncovers the *Challah* which is a special braided bread for Shabbath. The father then recites a blessing over the bread. After the recitation, he breaks off a piece of bread, dips it into salt and eats it. He then breaks off a piece for everyone at the table—the pieces are passed, and each person dips his piece of Challah into salt. It is then eaten in silence.

Salt Covenant

Salt was a necessary ingredient of daily food, and all sacrifices offered required salt (**Lev. 2:13**). So, there was a close connection between salt and covenant making. The two became intertwined. The common expressions of *"Salt between us"* or *"He has eaten of my salt"* conveyed the idea that if you ate a meal with someone you became related or united through the common salt in the meal. In **Numbers 18:19**, the heave offering is referred to by the Lord as covenant of salt forever.

In the New Testament in **Mark 9:50**, Christians are exhorted to, *"Have salt in yourselves, and have peace with one another."*

While we are on the subject of salt, it is helpful to remember that in antiquity the salt was not processed in the way our salt is today. Salt was bought in a clump like a rock. It was used by chipping away at the rock until the remaining minerals were reached; then it was no longer useful and was thrown out. Earlier in the same verse in Mark it reads, *". . . but if the salt have lost its saltiness, wherewith will you season it?"* In **Matthew 5: 13**, Jesus tells us (we Christians) that we *". . . are the salt of the earth, but if the salt has lost its savor . . . it is thenceforth good for nothing, but to be cast out, and to be trodden under foot of men."*—which is exactly what was done with a clump of salt that was no longer salty but had residual mineral content.

Meal

The Evening of the Sabbath meal is always a special meal. It is a time of family fellowship, a leisurely time of enjoyment.

Blessing after the Meal

After the meal, the left-over bread is again covered, and the food that is left is collected. The father then recites the final blessing—thanking God for the abundance of His provision.

Traditional Prayers

The traditional prayers that are recited by Jews were written by the Rabbis. The *Fence around the Law* found its way into the prayers. The reverence for the name of God, which was not spoken or written, separated the observant Jew from Father God. They became blinded by the *fence*. All Jewish prayers begin with, "*Blessed art thou Adoni, O King of the universe...*" When Jesus' disciples asked Him to teach them to pray, the Lord's Prayer began with "*Our Father...*" (Mt. 6:9 and Lk. 11:1-4).

The Going Out of the Sabbath

The Sabbath ends when three stars can be seen in the sky. There is another special service that marks the end of the Sabbath. Blessings are again said over wine. A candle is lit and extinguished by dipping it into the wine. Sweet smelling spices are passed around for everyone to smell. The spices are intended to refresh them, because they are saying goodbye to the Sabbath.

Goodbye to the Sabbath for another week. The First day of the week begins on what we consider to be Saturday night. In Israel, the streets become alive with the end of the Sabbath. It is a time for visiting friends or going to coffee shops. During the time of the disciples, this would have been the time when the believers gathered together on the first day of the week.

Commandments Concerning the Sabbath

Genesis 2:2 - Divine Example memorial to creation
Exodus 16:23-26 - collect manna on Friday for two days
Exodus 20:8-10 - and Deuteronomy 5:12-15; Commandment defined
Exodus 31:14-16 - death penalty
Exodus 35:2-3 - do not build a fire
Leviticus 16:31 - humble yourself
Leviticus 23:3, 24 - blowing trumpets

Leviticus 24:8 - showbread
Leviticus 25:2 - seventh year Sabbath rest
Numbers 28:9-10 - lambs offered
1 Chronicles 9:32 - Kohathites prepared showbread for the Sabbath
2 Chronicles 36: 19-21 - Babylonian captivity Sabbath rests

New Moon

Time Measured

- Days

    As has been mentioned several times already in Jewish thought, and according to scripture, a day goes from sunset to sunset. In Genesis throughout the creation account, we read "... *and the evening and the morning were the first day...*" and so on. Before the Babylonian captivity, the Hebrew day was divided morning, midday, and evening. In Babylon, they adopted the division into twelve hours (Jn. 11:9).

    On average, the first hour corresponds with 6am, the second hour with 9AM. There were three night watches. The first watch was until midnight; the second until 3AM (when the cock would crow); the third was from 3AM in the morning until 6AM.

- Weeks

    There is now, and has been from the time of Genesis, seven day weeks. The Biblical days were numbered not named. The sixth day ends at sundown and in the evening the Sabbath begins.

- Months

    The Jewish month is a lunar month, thus the appearance of the new moon is of great practical importance, and is observed as the New Moon Day. In Biblical times, the new moon was observed and authoritatively settled by the Sanhedrin, then made known to the Jews.

Fires were built on hilltops to announce the New Moon. The Samaritans started to build fires days earlier to confuse the Jews. In response to the confusion caused by the Samaritans swift runners were used as messengers in a type of relay until a Systematic calculation was begun.

The Jewish calendar was based on 29 days of lunation

Names of the Months

From the Canaanite times only four names have survived:
- Abib (Ex. 13:4)
- Ziv (first month) (1 Ki. 6:1)
- Ethanim (1 Ki. 8:2)
- Bul (1 Ki. 6:38)

The latter names are of Babylonian origin after exile:
1. Nisan (Neh. 2:1, Est. 3:7)
2. Iyar (not named in scripture)
3. Sivan (Est. 8:9)
4. Tammuz (Ez. 8:14)
5. Av (not mentioned in scripture)
6. Elul (Neh. 6:15)
7. Tishrei (not in scripture)
8. Marheshvan or merely Heshwan or Cheshvan (not mentioned in scripture)
9. Kislev (Zech. 7:1, Neh. 1:1)
10. Tevet or Tebeth (Est. 2:16)
11. Shevat or Shehath (Zechariah)
12. Adar (Ezra 6:15, Est. 3:7, 8:12)
13. Second Adar or We'Adar

Twelve lunar months equal 354 days, the calculation of the month was determined by the Sanhedrin. The New Year is in the month of Tishrei. This is interesting because the Lord told the children of Israel that the fourteenth of Abib was to be for them a new year.

Year

The Jewish calendar is dated from the creation of the world: 3760. You can calculate the Jewish year by adding 3761 to the number of the current year.

There are two time measuring-cycles: the Sun, which gives a year with 365 days; and a leap year every four years when February 29 is added. Using the lunar measuring-cycle gives a year with 354.37. The Jewish calendar adds a month, known as the Second Adar.

The lunar calendar is set on a nineteen year cycle.

New Moon

In Biblical times, the trumpet was blown over burnt offerings.

Two witnesses reported to the Jewish High Court: Sanhedrin Beit Din, after questioning and the matter was satisfied, the "sanctification of the new moon" followed. The sanctification of the new moon had to be made according to an eye witness report.

- **Numbers 28:11-15** - musaf sacrifice (additional)
- **1 Samuel 20:18** - festive meal
- **Amos 8:5** - no business transactions
- **2 Kings 4:23** - visit the prophet
- **Hosea 2:13** - joy of the new moon
- **Isaiah 66:23** - redemption (beautiful)

Today the New Moon is announced in the synagogues the Sabbath before.

In rabbinical writings and traditions, the rabbis have given women a day off because "they did not give their jewelry to make the golden calf".

"Also in the day of your gladness, ... and in the beginnings of your months, you shall blow the trumpets over your burnt offerings ... for a memorial..." **(Num. 10:10)**.

On the new moon, observing Jews recite "Half of the Hallel" repeating **Psalm 118:24** (Hallel Psalms are 113-118). *Ya'aleh ve Yavo* is inserted in the daily prayers and in the Grace after meals. The Torah reading of the day is **Numbers 28:1-2**.

The holy days of the month are dependent upon the New Moon which gives the New Moon an important place in the observance of Judaism.

Rabbinical Writings and Thoughts

Rabbi Hillel the Prince, last of the princes in the line of David, calculated the lunar calendar until the year 6,000 (which is 2240 in the standard calendar used today), and stopped because he believed that the Messiah would come in that year.

It is written in Jewish sources concerning the New Moon that it emerges from darkness and the New Moon is renewed. No one is so perfect that they will not fall—make mistakes, etc. Getting back up takes time, sometimes weeks, just as it takes weeks for a moon to become full. Yet there is slow steady growth, so it is in life. We frequently make mistakes, yet we continue to grow and develop towards maturity.

Pilgrim Feasts

The Pilgrim Feasts are those feasts that require the males of Israel to make a pilgrimage to worship at the Temple in Jerusalem. These feasts are: Passover, Feast of First Fruits and the Feast of the Tabernacles. The laws concerning these feasts are found in **Leviticus 23**. In previous chapters, Passover and the Feast of Unleavened Bread have been discussed; suffice it to say here that Passover begins the year of the Jewish religious calendar. So, in listing the feasts in order, the first pilgrim feast is Passover which is connected with the Feast of Unleavened Bread, the First Fruits and Pentecost.

Before beginning with the First Fruits, it will be helpful to remember that the Passover is a memorial meal in remembrance of the Angel of Death passing over the children of Israel the night the first born of Egypt were slain. For Christians, the ritual meal became what is known as communion, and we do this in remembrance of Jesus the Lamb, who was slain for us. The Feast of the Unleavened Bread (leaven is symbolic of sin), the bread without leaven is symbolic for us as the life we have covered by the blood of Jesus, where there is no condemnation for sin. The Holy Communion service is a reminder of this *truth*. This brings us to the next holy day, The First Fruits, which is symbolic of the resurrection of Jesus Christ.

First Fruits

"And the Lord spoke unto Moses, saying, speak to the children of Israel, and say unto them; when you come into the land which I give to you and you shall reap a harvest, then you shall bring a sheaf of the first fruits of your harvest unto the priest: and he shall wave the sheaf before the Lord... (**Lev. 23:9-10**).

The barley is the first to be harvested in Israel, and the harvest is at the time of Passover. Traditionally, the sheaf that was to be offered was cut the day before the Passover and was offered on the second day of the feast. The general harvesting took place between Passover and Pentecost.

Feast of Harvest-Shavuot - Counting the Omer

And you shall count unto you on the marrow after the Sabbath, from the day that you brought the sheaf of the wave offering; seven Sabbaths shall be complete "... *you shall number fifty days ... and you shall proclaim on the selfsame day, that it may be a holy convocation unto you ...* " (**Lev. 23:15-21**).

The *period of time between the wave offerings* on the day of First Fruits is known as *Counting the Omer*. The Hebrew word *omer* means *sheaf*. The counting marks the days between Passover and Pentecost. *Pentecost* is a Greek word that was used by the Hellenized Jews. It means *fifty*. The holy day is most commonly referred to as *Shavuot*. In Hebrew, Shavuot means *weeks* and is a reference to the counting of the weeks.

In Judaism, the holy day of Shavuot became associated with the giving of the Torah. The omer period began to symbolize the thematic link between Passover and Shavuot. It is believed that while the Passover celebrates the initial liberation of the Jewish people from slavery in Egypt, Shavuot marks the culmination of that process of liberation when the Jews became their own community with their own laws and standards. The counting of the omer is intended to remind the Jews mentally of the process of moving from slavery to freedom.

The day of the omer is changed at eight in the evening and a blessing is recited. The Omer Day of the Count is pronounced (for example), "Today is the sixth day of the omer." After six days, the number of weeks is added. "Today is the eighth day which is one week and one day of the omer."

Christians celebrate the Day of Pentecost in remembrance of the day the Holy Spirit was given to the disciples. It is interesting that the rabbis chose to celebrate this as the day of receiving the Law.

Feast of the Trumpets - Rosh ha Shanna
(or Rosh Hashanah)

"In the seventh month, in the first day of the month, you shall have a Sabbath, a memorial of blowing of trumpets . . . (Lev. 23:24).

The Feast of Trumpets has become known in Judaism as Rosh Hashanah, which literally means the head of the year or New Year. Obviously, this was the creation of rabbinical writings since there is no mention of this in the Bible. It is clear in the verse from Leviticus that the blowing of the trumpets was to take place on the first day of the seventh month, not the first month.

According to rabbinical writings, this is the anniversary of the creation of Adam and Eve, and also the anniversary of Abraham binding Isaac to offer him as a sacrifice. The sounding of the shofar is a call to repentance, as Yom Kippur is approaching. Also, there are special prayers that can be said near a body of water to evoke the verse that states, "... *and You shall cast their sins into the depths of the sea.*"

For Christians, this has a special meaning in regard to the coming of the Lord. *"For the Lord Himself shall descend from heaven with a shout, with the voice of the archangel, and with the trump of God; and the dead in Christ shall rise first. Then we which are alive and remain shall be caught up together with them in the clouds, to meet the Lord in the air...* (**1 Th. 4:16**). This is speaking of what we in the church call the rapture. The trumpet of God will sound and we will be caught up with Him!

Day of Atonement - Yom Kippur

The days between Rosh Ha Shanna and Yom Kippur are known as the Days of Awe. Since the destruction of the temple, the Jews have observed Yom Kippur as a day of affliction through fasting. In **Leviticus 16**, the detailed instructions are given for the keeping of this day when the temple was still in Jerusalem. Also in **Numbers 29:7-11**, there are less detailed instructions for the sacrifices. Included in the instructions in **Leviticus 23** is the command for the children of Israel to afflict themselves on this day. It is from **Leviticus 23** that the Jews today afflict their souls through fasting.

Kol Nidre

Kol Nidre is a declaration in Aramaic which (translated) means *all vows*. It is a declaration that nullifies all vows. This dates back to ancient Babylon when there was concern that evil spirits were able to embody the breath from words spoken, and if vows were not kept, they could exact dire consequences. Therefore, the declaration that "all vows past and from this Yom Kippur to the next" are null and void became a practice on the eve of Yom Kippur before the prayers for Yom Kippur were begun. The declaration pertains to vows made by the person to God. It does not relate to vows made with others.

In the 1880's, Jews in Europe suffered persecution because of this declaration so it was taken from the prayer book. Rabbis wrote different words to the melody, because the melody was a beloved part of Yom Kippur, but Cantors refused to sing the alternate words. In 1978, it was returned to the prayer book.

On Yom Kippur, the door to the synagogue closes, and then the cantor begins to sing the Kol Nidre. The cantor, choir, and congregation sing the Kol Nidre three times. The first time it is sung low, the second time it increases in volume and the third time is quite strong but not shouting. It is said that the three times is for past generations, present generation, and future generations.

Feast of Tabernacles - Succoth

"... *You shall dwell in booths seven days...* "

The Feast of Tabernacles is one of the three pilgrim feasts. It also has an agricultural significance in that it is the time of harvesting the fruit. It is celebrated for seven days. The first of the seven is a Shabbath rest day (**Lev. 23:39**). The second through the remaining days are known as Chol HaMoed. During these days, no heavy work is done. It is a time of visiting family, having special meals, and for the ritual daily walk around the synagogue carrying the four species.

FOUR SPECIES

The four species are Citron, Lulav (which is a palm branch), Myrtle branches and Willow branches tied together. These are carried around the synagogue. The seventh day is known as the Great Hoshanna. There are seven circuits that are made around the synagogue on this day, reciting **Psalm 118:25**, "*Save now ... O Lord! O Lord ... I pray send new prosperity.*" On the Shabbath that falls during the festival week, the book of Ecclesiastes is read in the synagogue.

WILLOW CEREMONY OF THE TEMPLE

The Mishna states that during the time of the Temple, Willow branches were piled around the altar and bending over the altar. The congregation circled the altar.

KINGS READ A PORTION OF TORAH

It was the custom during temple times for the king to read selected portions of the Torah during the Feast of Tabernacles. All the people would gather in the courtyard of the Temple to listen to the law being read (Dt. 31:10-11). It was during the feast of Sukkoth when the Jews, fed up with Alexander Jannai, pelted him with citrons.

EIGHTH DAY SOLEMN ASSEMBLY - SHEMINI ATZERET- SIMCHAT TORAH

"... *On the eighth day shall be an holy convocation unto you ... it is a solemn assembly; and you shall do no servile work therein*"(Lev. 23:36).

Outside of Israel this holy day, as well as all others except Yom Kippur, are celebrated for two days, so that all of Jewry, throughout the world, at some point in time over the two days will be celebrating together. For the Solemn Assembly, these two days are called Shemini Atzeret, which is the first and is celebrated with special prayer for rain. The second is Simchat Torah. Traditionally, Simchat Torah celebrates the conclusion of the cycle of the Torah reading. It is celebrated in the synagogue by carrying the scrolls, and marching and dancing around the synagogue.

REFERENCES

Buksbazen, V. (1954). *The Gospel in the Feasts of Israel.* W. Collingswood, NJ: The Friends of Israel.

Donn, H. H. (1972). *To be a Jew.* New York, NY: Basic Books, Inc., Publishers.

Harrison, R.K. (Ed.) (1988). *The new Unger's Bible dictionary.* Chicago, IL: Moody Press.

Strong, J. (1947). *Strong's exhaustive concordance of the Bible.* Nashville, TN: Thomas Nelson Publishers.

CHAPTER SEVENTEEN

JUDAISM & THE EARLY CHURCH

DISCUSSION QUESTION: Why should we study Church history?

Nazarenes

The earliest Jewish believers called themselves followers of "The Way" or Disciples. Their opponents called them "Nazarenes" (Acts 24:5). Tertullus, when informing the governor against Paul, referred to him as "... *a ringleader of the sect of the Nazarenes...*" In **Matthew 2:23**, we are told that Jesus dwelt in the city of Nazareth fulfilling the prophecies that "... *He shall be called a Nazarene....*" Some scholars believe the term *Nazarenes* actually comes from the verse in **Isaiah 11:10** where the Messiah is referred to as the "... *root of Jesse* ..." The Hebrew word for *root* is *netzer*. Whatever the origin, the name Nazarenes referred to all Jewish followers who had accepted Jesus as their Messiah until Paul and Barnabas went to Antioch and established a church. It was in Antioch that the followers of Jesus were first called *Christians* (Acts 11:26).

Early Disciples

The early disciples were, in fact, Jews who believed that Jesus was the promised Messiah. They continued to attend services at the local synagogues, and to practice the keeping of the Holy Days. On the day of Pentecost, they were in Jerusalem. *"And when the day of Pentecost was fully come, they were all with one accord in one place"* (**Acts 2:1**). We know from elsewhere in scripture that they attended regular services and kept the Sabbath. They gathered on the first day of the week, which was Saturday evening after the Sabbath ended. Until around 57 AD, they were considered to be a sect of Judaism. By that time, the Nazarenes and the mainline Jewish community were in conflict on a level that was beyond their belief in Jesus as the Messiah.

Followers of "The Way" expected Jesus to return. They lived communally and spent much of their time in prayer and the study of the scriptures. They were aware that the temple was to be destroyed and understood this to be a part of the "end times". Therefore, they were not interested in becoming involved with the Jews' rebellions against Rome. Due to persecution, they began to leave Jerusalem for Pella of the Decapolis, and to the Galilee area. When the Nazarenes refused to join in the revolts against Rome, the Jews excommunicated them. They were no longer considered a *sect*. The Jews added a *blessing* to the 18 blessings recited three times every day. This *blessing* is known as the *Birkat haMinim*. While it is called the blessing of the heretics—it is actually a *curse*:

> "For the apostates let there be no hope. And let the arrogant government be speedily uprooted in our days. Let the NOZERIM and the minim be destroyed in a moment. And let them be blotted out of the Book of Life and not inscribed together with the righteous, Blessed art thou oh Lord who humblest the arrogant."

The word *Nozerim* is actually Nazarene. During the middle ages, the word Nozerim was expunged from the Jewish prayer rites.

Church history began on the Day of Pentecost. It was a Jewish movement, but by 60 AD, they were separated from Judaism.

Rome and the Jews

Israel remained a Roman province and most of the Jews resented the Roman occupation. There was continuous unrest and frequent rebellions. One of the many ways the Romans demonstrated their authority over the Jews was by taking possession of the priestly robes. The procurator of Judea kept the priestly robes under lock and key, and if the high priest was not submissive, the Romans would refuse to give the high priest the priestly garments needed for Yom Kippur. Rome also maintained soldiers within the temple area.

Many of the Roman officials were corrupt. In fact, it was assumed by Rome that the Precepts (later called Procurators) would increase their wealth at the expense of those they governed. So common was this practice that there was an expression for it, *"philos tou kaisaros"* which means *to enrich personally.*

Political Rivalry among the Jews

There was political and economic rivalry between Jews and non-Jew pagans. The pagans made up about fifty percent of the population. Included in this group were the Romans who were officials or military stationed in Israel. Herod Agrippa was appointed king of northern Israel by Gaius Caligula. His kingdom was enlarged by Emperor Claudius to include Judea and Samaria. At times he favored the Jews. He had a work project to repave the roads in Jerusalem in order to provide work for the Jews. In spite of this, he was not trusted by the Jews, and he ultimately supported Rome.

The Hellenistic Jews were learned men, who thought in terms of developing Jerusalem economically. The Pharisees provided discipline within the context of the synagogue and embraced the Oral Law. The Sadducees did not accept the

Oral law. Each of these competing ideas and groups were constantly trying to influence others to support their position. The Essenes, on the contrary, lived a monastic life and just wanted to be left alone.

The zealots never gave up the dream of Israel again becoming an independent country under self-rule. They believed they could win a war against Rome with the help of the Jews living throughout the Roman Empire joining them in their revolt, and with the aid of the Parthians. They believed they would be able to recruit a large army from within Israel and that the timing was perfect because Rome was on the verge of a civil war.

Final Cause

Florus, the Procurator, robbed the temple in 66 AD. Among the crowd of Jews in Jerusalem, someone started passing a basket for donations for "poor Florus". This was an insult that could not be ignored. Florus loosed his soldiers on the population and thousands were killed. In retaliation, the zealots convinced the priests to refuse to offer the sacrifice on behalf of non-Jews, which in effect ended the sacrifices made for the emperor. This meant the refusal of allegiance to Rome.

The aristocrats (Hellenized Jews), whose well-being was tied to Rome, sent messengers to Florus and Agrippa asking for aid against those revolting Jews. The army marched in and captured the city of Jerusalem—but not the temple. In retaliation, the Jews in the city burned the Roman archives and the palace of Agrippa.

With the population of Jerusalem now united in the rebellion, the soldiers were losing the war. They surrendered and gave up their weapons. The Jews murdered them. This instigated the pagan cities to turn on the Jews. There was a massacre of Jews in Caesarea and in Alexandria. Again, Rome made an effort to take Jerusalem under the command of Cestuis Gallus but failed. This gave the Jews added momentum, another victory against Rome!

Josephus

With most of the Jewish population throughout Israel united in the war against Rome, even the middle class had joined in the rebellion. Only the aristocrats maintained their loyalty to Rome. The Jews now formed their own government from the middle class, and prepared to fortify the Galilee since Rome would come from the north. The middle class leaders sent a man named Josephus, who was a descendent of Matthias, to the Galilee to prepare for war. Josephus was in favor of self-rule but feared Rome—he wanted to play both sides. As a result of his double mindedness, he did not suitably prepare the Galilee.

Vespasian was appointed by Nero to take care of the rebellion in the east. He was given three highly trained legions. In addition, he received support from several Syrian kings; his forces totaled over 60,000. Because of Josephus' deliberate effort to assist Rome, the Galilee was defeated. Josephus escaped to a cave and later was attached to the Roman General with the assignment of weakening the morale of the Jews. He wrote all of this in what we know as the history of Flavius Josephus.

With Galilee defeated, the support the Jews hoped would come from Parthia, and the Jews throughout the empire, did not come. Following Nero's death, Vespasian returned to Rome to lead the empire. His son Titus was left to finish the task of taking Jerusalem and putting down the Jewish uprising for good.

Because Josephus was a traitor, who had been sent to the Galilee by the middle-class government, the zealots killed all those in government. A civil war began in Jerusalem. The moderates held the city and the zealots had the temple. The zealots called for help from the Idumeans (who at that time had become ardent Jewish patriots). They came in the dead of the night and slaughtered the moderates. The zealots assumed command. There were also rival groups among the patriots who constantly fought each other. The result was that the zealots weakened their own position with their infighting.

Vespasian and Titus waited patiently for the Jews to self-destruct.

Under Titus's command, the Romans made camp on Mt. Scopus. The rivals ceased fighting each other and united against Rome, but it was too late. The Roman siege began. Titus would not allow civilians to leave Jerusalem, placing a burden on the limited supplies in the city. The sacrifices continued in the temple, until there was nothing left to sacrifice. The sacrifices ended on the 17th of Tammuz, which is still observed as a fast day by observant Jews. On the 9th of Ab, three weeks later, Titus ordered the gates of the temple to be set on fire, ending the siege victoriously. The competition among the Jewish religious leaders had been the cause of this final conflict which led to the conquest by Rome. The Jews were dispersed and Israel was renamed Palestine. The population was a mix of Jews, Christians, and pagans at this time. The population of this geographical area became known as Palestinians. The name was derived from the ancient enemy of Israel, the Philistines, who were descendants of the Caphtorim mentioned in Genesis 10:14.

Triumphal Procession

Seven hundred Jewish captives were forced to march in the triumphal procession in Rome. The Arch of Titus still stands in commemoration of when the procession first came in sight. Coins of the time were inscribed *"Judea Capta"—Judea has been taken.*

Early Church

The followers of Jesus had been spread abroad as a result of Rome's dominance and this provided an excellent opportunity to take the gospel to the ends of the earth. The pagan world believed in magic, astrology, myths and heroes who were elevated to divine status. What was extraordinary about the Christians' claim was that it happened now in the land of Israel. Jesus was born of a virgin in Judea, crucified under Pontius

Pilate, and rose from the dead, all in recent history. Gentiles were attracted to monotheism, Jewish morality, the sacred books, the stable family, the charity that Jews practiced. In addition, Judaism was a religion of a book, in a way no other ancient religion was. For example, the reconstruction of the Israelite society after Babylonian captivity had been firmly based on the Law of Moses.

Around the synagogues there were gathered "God-fearers"—from among these came the first Christian converts. The Septuagint became the authorized version of the scriptures used by the early Gentile Church. In **Acts 15**, the first **Church Council** decided what was required of Gentile Believers.

By 175 BC there were Jewish communities throughout Mesopotamia, North Africa and India. These communities had synagogues, and it was to these synagogues that the disciples would go to share the Good News of the Messiah. The "God-fearers" (gentile believers) soon outnumbered the Jews.

There was a difference in interest and focus of Jewish Believers in Israel and Gentile Believers in the Greco-Roman world. For example, the first generation of believers in Israel expected the Lord to return in glory at any time. There was a strong interest in Messianic prophecy. In the Greek world, the dominate speculative interest was in the beginning of things, the focus was on the wisdom of God in creation, pre-existent from eternity, the inherent power by which He holds the cosmos in place, the inherence (indwelling) of the Lord within His church, the universal church as described in Ephesians, all Christians being united to one another through baptism (One Body).

When Jerusalem was destroyed in 70 AD, and when in 135 AD, Hadrian expelled the Jews from Judea and renamed Jerusalem Aelia Capitolina and Israel Palestine, there was an emancipation of Gentile Christendom from its Jewish roots. Gentile believers outnumbered Jewish believers in the Mediterranean world. They could look for continuity with the apostles, not only to the churches of the east, but also to Rome where Peter and Paul were martyred.

The Nazarenes continued in existence through the fourth century. They were few in numbers and were restricted geographically to pockets of settlements along the eastern shore of the Mediterranean. From their documents, they seem to have been developing Christological in the same vein as the church; they were also developing a doctrine on the Holy Spirit. By the fourth century, they were excluded from the church, because they continued with circumcision and the keeping of the Sabbath on Saturdays.

Church Unity

The unity in the early church depended on two issues: the rite of baptism, and the meeting on Sunday for Thanksgiving and Communion. The rite of baptism had its roots in the bath necessary for all converts to Judaism from paganism. For the Christian, it involved a Statement of Faith, which was concerned mostly with statements about Christ's person taken from **Acts 8:37**, "... *I believe that Jesus is the Son of God.*" and from **Matthew 28:19** "... *baptizing them in the name of the Father, and of the Son, and of the Holy Ghost.*" The Apostles Creed derives from the creed used for baptism during the second century in Rome. The first part of the Sunday Service consisted of Psalms, readings of scripture and prayers. The Christian Sunday was not made a *Day of Rest* until Constantine decreed it in 321 AD.

It became necessary to establish the authority for doctrines because many false teachings were arising. The first steps taken were by Ignatius of Antioch when he insisted on a local bishop (God's representative on earth) as the focus of unity, and that sacraments could not be administered without a bishop. By 185 AD, the gradual formation of the New Testament canon was complete. The Rule of Faith, which was a summary of the main events in the redemptive process, was also completed. Within two generations, there was a transition from apostles, prophets, and teachers, to bishops, presbyters (priests) and deacons.

The churches that were established by traveling missionaries became local and stationary with clergy. As the churches consolidated, the part played by traveling missionaries receded into the background.

Church Councils - Acts 15

From the time of the apostles, it became common to hold local church councils which were attended by all the bishops in the province. The church structure consisted of Bishops, Elders and Pastors. By the time of Constantine, these councils had widened in scope and included bishops of several provinces. It was necessary for Christians to be able to define and explain what they believed to a sophisticated Greco-Roman world. Church Councils had the task of formulating the doctrines of the church.

Discussion and Issues of the Early Church

The discussions at the church councils included the following: What is the difference between "essence" and "energies"? Orthodoxy distinguishes between God's "essence" and His "energies". His *Essence* is unapproachable, whereas His *Energies* come down to us, and permeate all His creation. We experience His *Energies* in the form of deifying grace and divine light.

Another important discussion related to what we today call *the Trinity*. In the discussions, it was explained that God is a personal trinity in three persons, each of whom dwells in the other two, a perpetual movement of love, eternal movement of love, and perpetual radiance. Union with God is union with Divine Energies.

- **Hypostasis.** Used by Aristotle in contrast to Plato to speak of the "objective reality of a thing or its inner reality" (as opposed to outer form or illusion). In early Christian writings, it is used to denote being or substantive reality.

- **Ousia.** Being (from an ancient Greek noun formed on the feminine present participial of *eivai* (to be). The generally agreed upon meaning of Ousia in Eastern Christianity is—all that subsists by itself and which has not its being in another.
- **Three Hypostases in One Ousia.** Three object realities in one being is the orthodox doctrine of the Holy Trinity.
- **Filioque** (Latin). Spirit proceeds from the Father and the Son.

Other important topics were: What is a *theocosmic* relationship: Revelation is a theocosmic relationship which includes us.

The concept of *logos* needed to be defined: the *logos* (essential reason) in regard to creation. *Exnihilo*: before creation nothing existed outside of God, every created thing has its logos, "its essential reason".

Logos had become a technical term in philosophy, beginning with Heraclitus (557—475 BC). He used the term for *the principal of order and knowledge*. It was further developed by the Sophists to apply to discourse, and then by Aristotle to mean *reasoned discourse*. To the Stoic, it was *the divine animating principal pervading the universe*.

The Gospel of John identifies the Logos through which all things are made as divine and further identifies *Jesus* as the *incarnation of the Logos*.

Further Discussions of the Early Church Fathers

- **Time and Eternity:** The *Beginning* is a sort of instantaneousness, non-temporal occurrence in and of itself, but whose creative explosion gives rise to time—a point of contact with the Divine Will is what will henceforth become and endure. Origin of creation is a change, a "beginning"; time is a form of created being, eternity belongs to God.

- **Uncreated Grace** as it relates to *the soul of man*: This means that "uncreated grace" is implicated in the creative act itself, and that the soul receives, simultaneously—life and grace—for grace is the breath of God, "the current of divinity," the vivifying presence of the Holy Spirit. The grace of the Holy Spirit is the real principal of our existence.
- **Diophysitism:** literally means *two natures*; body and divine in harmony; dual nature, divine and human, united perfectly.
- **Homoousios** is *one substance* or *of one essence*: This term was formulated at the first council in 325 BC to affirm that God the Son and the Father are the same substance.
- **Monarchianism** declares: that God is *one person*; denies the trinity.
- **Theotokos** means: *God-bearer, Birth-Giver of God*; a less literal translation is *Mother of God*.
- **Iconoclasm** refers to: Image breaking, ban on religious images.
- For further study: Ecumenical Councils

Armenian Apostolic Church

The apostles, Thaddeus and Bartholomew, are accredited with preaching the gospel in Armenia. Christianity gradually rooted there and in 310 AD became the official religion of Armenia following the conversion of king Tiridates. This is the first Christian nation in history.

Assyrian Orthodox Church

In 1 Peter 5:13, the elect church in Babylon is mentioned, indicating that the apostles had preached the gospel in Babylon.

The Assyrian Orthodox Church was established by the apostles: Thomas, Thaddeus, and Bartholomew in the first century.

Jonah was called to Nineveh and the city repented. Is it possible his ministry, and their repentance, laid the foundation for the first Christian nation and first organized church?

Persecuted Church - Diocletian

Diocletian (303 AD) led the Greatest Persecution of Christians.

He divided the empires of the East and West. The church in the west became known as the Latin Church, and the church in the east became known as the Orthodox Church as a result of this division of the empire.

Constantine

Constantine converted to Christianity in 312 AD. He moved the capital to the east and built a new city, Constantinople. This is significant because there were no previous temples to pagan gods. This was the first Christian city. In 331 AD, Constantine commissioned Eusebius to deliver 50 Bibles to the church in Constantinople (this may have provided the motivation for the cannon list). He called the first church council in 325 AD known as the Council of Nicaea. Constantine was baptized in 337 AD.

The following is the order of the Seven Church Councils and a listing of the topics discussed.

Council of Nicaea

The Council of Nicaea represented the first effort to obtain a consensus in the church through an assembly representing all of Christendom. There had been differences within the church on the various doctrines developed by the previous church councils. Constantine wanted there to be a unified definition (agreed upon by all the church) of the doctrinal issues.

The main accomplishments of this council were: the settlement of the Christological issues of the nature of God, the Son and His relationship to God the Father, the construction of the first part of the Creed of Nicaea, settled the calculation of the date of Easter, and the promulgation of canon law. This established a precedent for subsequent local and regional councils of Bishops (Synods) to create statements of belief and cannons of doctrinal orthodoxy.

Within the early Christian communities there was a debate on the divinity of Christ. The council confirmed and defined what it believed to be the teachings of the apostles regarding who Christ is—that Christ is the one true God in Deity with the Father.

An agreement was reached on:
- Easter/Pasch was celebrated at the same time as the Jewish feast of Passover. The Christians were dependent upon the Jews annually to establish the date for Easter Sunday.
- It was decided to calculate the date, for all of the church to celebrate together on the same day, using the Julian calendar.
- The Minimum term for instruction for Baptism.
- Ordination of a bishop.
- Prohibition of self-castration
- Annual synods twice a year provincial
- Probation of usury among the clergy.

Second Ecumenical Council: First Council of Constantinople

The Second Council was held in Constantinople in 381 AD. It was called by Theodosius I and Gregory Nazianzus to unite all Christendom. This Second Council:
- Expanded and adapted the Nicene Creed (online: Comparison between the Creed of 325 and the Creed of 381 which includes an Article on the Holy Spirit).
- Holy Spirit affirmed to be God.

- Seven cannons dealing with administration (only 4 accepted by Rome).
- Third Canon (famous) gave Bishop of Constantinople prerogative and honor after the Bishop of Rome.

The previous debates had been on the Son, Second Person of the Trinity. By 381 AD, the Third Person, the Holy Spirit, became a topic of debate.

Third Ecumenical Council: Ecumenical Council of Ephesus 431 AD

The debate at this council was on:
- Christ's human and divine natures (Nesotorians).
- Theotokos (God-bearer, Mother of God) vs. Christotokos (Birth-giver of Christ).
- Political (refused to recognize each other).
- Decided Mary to be called Theotokos (dispute continued; settled in 1994).
- Eight cannons.
  - 1-5 condemned heretics.
  - 6 - excommunicate those who do not accept decrees.
  - 7 - condemned departure from creed of 325 AD.
  - 8 - authority of bishops.

This council resulted in major schism.

Fourth Ecumenical Council: Council of Chalcedon 553 AD

- Clear statement of the human and divine natures of Christ.
- 28 cannons (27 were disciplinary).

Fifth Ecumenical Council: Second Council of Constantinople 680—681 AD
- Hypostatic Union of Christ.

Sixth Ecumenical Council: Third Ecumenical Council of Constantinople 680—681 AD
- Human and Divine Will of Jesus.
- Christ's individual actions were directed by His divine-will, His human-will nevertheless possessed true spontaneity in virtue of its intrinsic drive to obey its Creator.

Seventh Ecumenical Council: Second Council of Nicaea 787 AD
- Veneration of icons

Byzantine Empire

The Byzantine Empire is the name given to the continuation of the Roman Empire which converted to Christianity and used Greek as its principal language. This flourished in the eastern Mediterranean for more than 1,000 years until its fall in 1453. The name Byzantine is derived from Byzantium, the city which Constantine I made his new capital and renamed Constantinople, (presently) Istanbul, Turkey.

324—610 AD

The foundation of Constantinople, and the final division of the empire into western and eastern parts occurred during this period. Christianity became the most favored religion. The rise of the heresies of Arianism, Nestorianism, and Monophysitism plagued the church.

610—1081 AD

It was during this period of history that we see the rise of Islam. Muhammad (570—632 AD) established the system of forced conversion, with the exception of "the people of the book" (Jews and Christians) who were *demis* (half persons). In 634 AD, Muslim Arabs seized Palestine and Jerusalem.

From 726 to 870 AD, Christians disputed over theological formulas, iconoclasm, etc. ending in the Great Schism—dividing the Orthodox Church of the East from the Latin (Roman Catholic) Church of the West.

1081—1453 AD

There was continued conflict between Latin and Orthodox Churches. In 1095, the Crusades began lasting until 1291. The Crusades were religiously motivated; the crusaders emblem was the cross. The name *crusaders* or *crusade* was taken from the French word that means take up your cross. The first crusade was to regain access to the holy places in and near Jerusalem.

Crusaders

Pope Urban II called for a great expedition to free Jerusalem from the Seljuk Turks. The first Crusade established a Western Christian military presence in the Near East. The Latin Kingdom of Jerusalem was established by Godfrey of Bouillon. Three other Crusader states were established: Tripoli, Antioch, and Edessa. Godfrey of Bouillon is also known as "Defender of the Holy Sepulcher."

There were two Military Orders: the **Templers** who guarded the Temple of the Lord, and the **Hospitaliers** who were attached to the hospitals which the crusaders built.

During the time of the crusades, Latin Christians were considered superior and the indigenous Orthodox Christians were restricted access to the holy sites and were oppressed. The crusaders lived in castles and cities. The local population was farmers and lived in the countryside. The crusaders failed to understand the importance of being connected with the rest of the Byzantine territory. They depended on the Latin kingdoms and failed to unite the Byzantine territories. Within the crusades, there was much rivalry and treason. These are some of the reasons for their failure.

Christendom's continued internal conflict over the right of access to the holy sites resulted in the Status Quo Laws being enforced in the Holy Land.

Status Quo

Status Quo is a Latin term and is defined as the existing condition or state of affairs. In other words, the way things are. In International Law it denotes a situation, actual or legal, that exists or once existed and whose reinstatement or preservation is in question. In the Holy Land, it refers to a firman issued by the Ottoman Sultan Abdulmecid I on February 8, 1852 to freeze conditions of ownership and responsibility as a legal framework to resolve disputes concerning the church of the Holy Sepulcher, the Tomb of Mary, and the Church of the Nativity.

According to the Status Quo:

- The Franciscans are considered the Custodians of the Holy Places, because this was the appointment of Pope Clement VI in 1342.
- The Greek Orthodox Patriarch is the official representative of the whole Christian community as was determined at the beginning of the Ottoman Empire in 1463.
- The Armenian Church has a special place alongside the Catholics and the Orthodox because of a declaration by the Sultan in 1829 in gratitude for Armenian service to the Empire (later Armenian genocide).
- According to the Status Quo, two Muslim families- Nusseibah and Judeh-hold the key to the Holy Sepulcher and ceremoniously unlock the doors each morning and lock them each evening.
- The Coptic Church has a place on the backside of the Tomb of Christ.

- The Syrian Church has a place in the Chapel of Joseph of Arimathea and Nicodemus in a room hidden away on the perimeter.
- The Ethiopian Church has a place in a humble mud hut compound on the roof.
- Anglicans and Lutherans are not included in the Church of the Holy Sepulcher because they showed up later.

No government will ever change the Status Quo laws.

☙

REFERENCES

Booty, J. (1979). *The Church in history.* New York, NY: The Seabury Press.

Chadwick, H. (1993). *The early Church.* Middlesex, UK: Penguin Books.

Ferguson, E. (2003). *Backgrounds of early Christianity.* Grand Rapids, MI: Wm. B. Eerdmans Publishing Company.

Pritz, R. A. (1987). *Nazarene Jewish Christianity: From the end of the New Testament period until its disappearance in the fourth century.* Jerusalem, IL: The Magnes Press.

Ware, T. (1997). *The Orthodox Church.* New York, NY: Penguin Books.

CHAPTER EIGHTEEN

MODERN ISRAEL

DISCUSSION QUESTION: Should all Jews live in Israel?

Zionism

The term Zionism was coined in 1890 by Nathan Birnbaum of Vienna. In 1893, he published a brochure titled: *The National Rebirth of the Jewish People in its Homeland as a Means of Solving the Jewish Question.* The general definition of Zionism is: *the national movement for the return of the Jewish people to their homeland and the resumption of Jewish sovereignty in the Land of Israel.* However, Theodor Herzl is credited as the founder of the Zionist movement.

Jewish communities throughout Europe, and eventually the United States, became increasingly committed to the establishment of a Homeland for the Jews in Palestine. Money was collected by local synagogues and sent to the national headquarters to purchase land in Palestine. Political pressure was applied when possible (an example is the Balfour Declaration).

Zionism is a Jewish doctrine and movement named after Zion, the hill in ancient Jerusalem, upon which the royal palace of King David was built. Zionism is a form of nationalism of Jews and Jewish culture that supports a Jewish Nation State in the territory defined as the Land of Israel. Zionism supports Jews upholding their Jewish identity, opposes assimilation of

Jews into other societies and advocates the return of Jews to Israel as a means for Jews to be a majority in their own nation and to be liberated from anti-Semitism and persecution.

Factors in the Development of Zionism

The pogroms of Europe were a significant factor in the development of Zionism. A *pogrom* is an organized massacre of a particular ethnic group, in this case, Jews in Europe who were frequent victims of such persecution. Zionism was birthed as a result of this and similar persecution that Jews throughout the world were experiencing.

Beliefs of Zionism

- Jews are a people/nation united by history. Theodor Herzl, "Jews are one people—our enemies have made us one".
- They have in common: persecution; corporate culture; economic socialism (Eastern European Jews); religion.
- There has been a loss of culture through the Diaspora.
- The solution is the ingathering of some Jews in the land of Israel.
- The goals to be carried out diplomatically.
- Begin by buying land in Palestine.
- Education.

Zionism arose and was embraced, in large part, due to the pogroms and anti- Semitism that plagued the Jews. The pogroms of the 1880s caused many young Jews to commit to the movement.

In 1862, **Moses Hess**, a Jew, published a book **Rome and Jerusalem** which advocated the return of Jews to Palestine, and the establishment of a spiritual center there. This was religious Zionism which called on Jews to return to Palestine for religious reasons. In 1881-82, **Hovevei Zion** (Lovers of Zion) groups sprang up soon after the pogroms. They organized the first Aliyah to Palestine.

In 1875-1927, **Ahad Ha'am** (thinker and writer) stressed the significance of maintaining a Jewish national culture, including developing Hebrew as a modern language. And in 1860-1904, **Theodor Herzl** gave a political dimension to the concept of Zionism. The pamphlet, "The Jewish State" (1896), argued for a Jewish homeland preferably in Palestine secured through international agreement. The British offered Uganda to the Jews for their Jewish state in 1897, but it was turned down by the 7th **Zionist Congress**.

With the failure of the Russian revolution of 1905, which was followed by repression and pogroms, the migration of Jewish youths to Palestine increased as did support for the Zionism movement among European Jews. Since many Russian settlers were socialists (Marxist and non-Marxist), there was a rise of socialist Zionism in Palestine.

Chaim Weizmann and **Nahum Sokolow** (1917-1922) played crucial roles in securing the **Balfour Declaration** from the British government (1917)—which was incorporated into Britain's League of Nations mandate over Palestine in 1922.

1917 BALFOUR DECLARATION

Dear Lord Rothschild:
I have much pleasure in conveying to you on behalf of His Majesty's Government the following declaration of sympathy with Jewish Zionist aspirations which has been submitted to, and approved by, the Cabinet. "His Majesty's Government view with favor the establishment in Palestine of a National Home for Jewish people, and will use their best endeavors to facilitate the achievement of this object, it being clearly understood that nothing shall be done which may prejudice the civil and religious rights of existing non-Jewish communities in Palestine, or the rights and political status enjoyed by

Jews in any other country". I should be grateful if you would bring this declaration to the knowledge of the Zionist Federation.

In 1896, at the **First Zionist Conference**, they created operative and executive bodies. However, the first immigration by Jews to Palestine preceded this conference.

ALIYAH
(*"To Rise"* is the word used for immigrant to Israel)

First Aliyah 1882—1904

- 30, 000 from Russia
- Agricultural work was done by Arabs, immigrants were more religious
- Achievements: Moshavat (little colonies)
    Petah Tekva
    Rosh Pina
    Metulla

Baron Edmond Rothschild, a well know benefactor from France, sent in experts to save the Moshavat. These experts took over and told them what to grow and when. The Moshavim Movement did not do well financially, but they were able to develop new settlements.

Second Aliyah 1905

- Socialist
- 30,000 different breed (factory workers)
- Problems with attitudes between First and Second Aliyah
- 1907 marked the beginning of the Kibbutz movement (training farms in Kinneret)

World War I - 1914—1918

Correspondence between the British High Commissioner in Egypt and Sharif Hussein of Mecca led to an agreement between the British and the Arabs on the establishment of an Arab kingdom in the Middle East in exchange for an Arab military revolt against the Ottomans. Arabs believed the Arab kingdom included Palestine. With the vision of an Arab Kingdom that included all the area known politically as the Province of Syria, the Arabs joined the United Kingdom, France and Russia against the Ottoman's.

1916 Sykes-Picot Agreement

The great powers of the West met and came to an Anglo-French agreement on how the Fertile Crescent was to be divided between Britain and France. This was followed by the Balfour Declaration in 1917. Since Palestine was known, since the times of the Romans, as Southern Syria, the Arabs were shocked and felt betrayed when the British issued the Balfour Declaration in 1917.

Arab Conference

At the end of the war there was a General Arab Conference held in Damascus. At this conference, the Arabs rejected the Balfour Declaration and declared that Palestine was considered part of Southern Syria.

THIRD ALIYAH 1919—1923

- 37,000 built on what the Second Aliyah began
- Haganah Defense (attacks from Arabs)

The First, Second and Third Aliyah were Russian Jews. The Second and the Third were the most influential.

1919 Arab Literary Club and Arab Club

These clubs were founded to propagate Arab nationalism. Al-Husseini appointed Grand Mufti of Jerusalem, and Muslim-Christian Associations formed to protest against the Balfour Declaration. The Arabs protested against the Balfour Declaration from 1918 to 1939.

Perhaps at this point, it would be convenient to define who is an Arab. The traditional definition is anyone whose mother tongue is Arabic is an Arab.

US Limits Immigration (rations) - 1924

The limits to immigration were taken from the 1890 Second Johnson-Reed Act which limited the annual number of immigrants who could be admitted from any country to 2% of the number of people from that country already living in the states. The law was aimed at further restricting Southern and Eastern Europeans (among them Jews) who had migrated in large numbers to escape persecution.

Fourth Aliyah 1924

- Poland 70,000
- Economic reasons (Jews represented 10% in Poland) discriminatory laws
- Economic crisis, more Jews leaving Israel than are coming

Creation of a Political Entity

- Jewish Agency 50-50 Zionist and non-Zionist; represented all Jews
- Vaad Leumi National Council; executive of Jewish population in Palestine, Parliament was called Assembly of Representatives
- Palestine was British, all Departments and Services were under the High Commissioner
- Jewish Political Parties played a role in ruling
  All parties had newspapers "party papers"
  Health funds
  Women's Organizations
  Youth Movement
  Settlements
  Labor Bureau
  Military Component
  Schools
- Haganah (Labor Party)
- Palmach (Labor)
- Irgun (Revisionists)

- Histadrut and Labor Union controlled Haganah
- Mapai (1930)

Mandate Period

At San Remo and Sevres in 1920, France and Britain set up a mandate system and divided the Middle East into the following mandates: Syria and what is known today as Lebanon was under the French Mandate. Iraq and Palestine (including what is now known as Jordan) came under the British Mandate. The Hijaz, Saudi Arabia, was to be independent. The Mandate for France and Britain was to assist these countries in becoming independent nations.

In 1922, Abdullah was given the territory east of the Jordan River known today as Jordan. In 1924, Sa'ud toppled Husayn in the Hijaz, Saudi Arabia. Faisal was appointed as new king of Iraq by Britain. Iraq gained independence in 1932.

Inside of Palestine, as the Jewish immigration continued and the Arabs protests were not successful, a war was raging between the Jews and the Arabs, both laying claim to the same land. In 1928—1929, following an incident at the Wailing Wall, Jewish worshippers brought benches and portioned areas for men and women. The Arabs retaliated by running a thoroughfare through the area. The clashes escalated and spread to Hebron and other areas until there was a full-on Arab Rebellion in Palestine.

Muslim Brotherhood

In 1928, the Muslim Brotherhood was established by Sheik Hasan al-Bana. The Brotherhood's charter rejects Western values and Communism. It calls for a Pan-Islamic state founded on the basis of Shari'ah ruled by Caliph, views Israel as an agent of the west, and the Koran is the constitution. A pan-Islamic state would include all of the province of Syria as defined by history.

White Paper

Britain sent a Commission of Inquiry to investigate the post-election violence in 1930, and a White Paper was issued by Lord Passfield blaming the Jewish Agency and Zionist land purchases from Arabs (some peasants became homeless) for the 1929 disturbances. Consequently, Britain put a limit on Jewish immigration.

Weizmann was so incensed by the report that he resigned from the leadership of the Jewish Agency. The British government then issued a letter explaining away the Passfield White Paper, which angered the Arabs. It taught the Arabs that the Zionist influence was strong enough to sway the British government.

The pan-Islamic Conference, which took place in Jerusalem in 1931, was an early warning to the Christian Arabs of the persecution that would follow, but many still had hope of a pan-Arab Middle East that would include Christians. The major Arab movements were: pan-Islamic, pan-Arab, and the Greater Syria Movement. None of these included a Jewish state in Palestine.

In 1936, the Arab Strike was led by al-Hajj Amin-al-Husayni, the leader of the Arab Higher Committee. This turned into a large scale rebellion. Again, the British government sent a commission of inquiry; the commission's report (in the form of another White Paper) was given by Lord Peel in 1937 and was opposed by the Arabs. The Peel Commission of 1937 called for Palestine to be partitioned. The partition was opposed by Arabs, and the Jews were not happy with it either because of the small allotment of land.

Yet another British White Paper in 1939 limited Jewish immigration, put restrictions on Jewish land purchases, and was actually a De facto withdrawal from the Balfour Declaration.

World War II

During WWII in Germany, the systematic slaughter of Jews swayed world sympathy in favor of the establishment of a homeland for the Jews in Palestine. The newly formed United

Nations voted to partition Palestine into two states, and in 1948, modern Israel came into existence.

War of Independence

The United Nations announced the partition on November 29, 1947. The Jewish underground (Irgun, Stern Gang) had concentrated all its efforts in driving the British out of Palestine since the favor of Britain was with the Arabs. In line with that effort, the first terrorist attack in Palestine was conducted by the Irgun in the bombing of the King David Hotel. These underground militias now had to confront the Arabs who were seeking to undo the UN decision.

According to Menachem Begin, the first counter-attacks were launched December 11—13. On December 20th, a bomb was placed by the Irgun at Damascus Gate in Jerusalem. It exploded killing 15 Arabs and wounding 50 others. Several days later, the Irgunists exploded a barrel bomb near Jaffa Gate, at a bus stop, killing 17 Arabs and wounding 50 more. These terrorist tactics have been copied and further developed by the Arabs. On January 9, 1948, Arabs attacked Jewish communities in northern Palestine. The British surrendered bases and arms to Arabs, but refused to allow the Jews to form a militia. The Jews were ill equipped to win a war against the united Arab countries that surrounded them.

The total number of Jewish immigrants between the years of 1922 and 1948 was approximately 480,000. By May 1948, the Jewish population in Palestine was 650,000. There were another 700,000 refugees from Arab countries that were absorbed by the fledgling nation.

From April 1 to May 14, the Haganah fought and captured Tiberias and Haifa—a significant gain. Israel became independent May 14, 1948, and the following day, five Arab armies from Egypt, Syria, Transjordan, Lebanon, and Iraq attacked Israel. In 1949, an Armistice was signed with Israel and four of the five invading countries. Egypt signed February 24, Lebanon signed on March 23, Jordan signed on April 3, and

Syria, the last to sign, on July 20. Iraq did not sign an agreement with Israel.

Population Transfer

A large portion of the Arab population fled their homes, expecting to return after their Arab brothers expelled the Jews. The first to leave were 30,000 wealthy Arabs. Six thousand left from Tiberias when Jewish forces seized the area, and 50,000 fled from Haifa. By the time the provisional government was in place 200,000 had left. At the end of the war and the time of setting up a Jewish government, there were between 450,000 to 600,000 Palestinian refugees. The United Nations Relief for Palestinian Refugees (UNRPR) was formed and continues to aid Palestinians to date (2014). About 160,000 Arabs remained in Israel.

Egypt controlled Gaza where 200,000 Palestinian residents were refused entry into Egypt. Syria declined to resettle 85,000 refugees. Jordan was the only Arab country that welcomed the Palestinians and granted them citizenship. Jordan annexed the West Bank and the Old City of Jerusalem.

Since its creation in modern history, Israel has never known a lasting peace. The lists of wars include: The Suez Canal (1956), Six Day War (1967), Yom Kippur War (1973), Israel and Lebanon (1983), the Intifada (1987), and following the first Intifada, there was a second, and to date the continuing war with Gaza.

REFERENCES

Bard, M. (1999). *The complete idiot's guide to the Middle East conflict*. Indianapolis, MN: Alpha Books.

Friedman, T. (1990). *From Beirut to Jerusalem*. New York, NY: HarperCollins Publisher.

Goldschmidt, A. Jr. (1996). *A concise history of the Middle East*. Boulder, CO: Westview Press.

Hiro, D. (1996). *Dictionary of the Middle East*. New York, NY: St. Martin's Press.

Hourani, A., Khoury, P. S. & Wilson, M. C. (Eds.). (1993). *The modern Middle East: A reader*. Berkley, CA: University of California Press.

Pipes, D. (1990). *Greater Syria: The history of an ambition*. New York, NY: Oxford Press.

Rolef, S. H. (Ed.) (1993). *Political dictionary of the State of Israel*. Jerusalem, IL: The Jerusalem Publishing House.

CHAPTER NINETEEN

PALESTINIANS and the ARAB-ISRAELI CONFLICT

DISCUSSION QUESTION: Who are the Palestinians?

Palestine-Southern Syria

Until 1920, Syria referred to a region that stretched from the borders of Anatolia to the borders of Egypt and from the edge of Iraq on to the Mediterranean Sea. This comprises what is known today as Syria, Lebanon, Israel, Jordan and the Gaza Strip plus Alexandretta. From Roman times, this area was known as the Province of Syria, and Palestine was known as Southern Syria or Palestine (Greater Syria). The Province of Syria was a remote province of an empire—Roman in antiquity and the Ottoman in recent history. With the defeat of the Ottoman Empire, the province was broken up into countries by Britain and France with the promise of becoming independent nations. It was assumed by the Palestinians and the Arab nations, that Palestine was included in that promise.

The United Nations' decision to partition Palestine for the establishment of a Jewish state was unacceptable to the Palestinians and the newly formed Arab states—whose interest was in territorial expansion, not the plight of the Palestinian people. The rejection of the proposed partition resulted in what the Arabs call the Disaster, and the Jews refer to as the War of Independence.

The Disaster (War of Independence)

In 1947, the population of Palestine was 1,810,037. Of these, fewer than ten percent were Christians. Between December of 1947 and April of 1948, the Palestinian-Arab community ceased to exist as a social and political entity. Over 350 Palestinian villages vanished. They were destroyed and the land was allocated to Jews. The Arab population of Jaffa dropped from 70,000 to 80,000 to 3,000 to 4,000. Between 500,000 and 1,000,000 Palestinians became refugees (The Palestinians, Kimmerling).

During the Mandate Period (1920—1947), Britain banned political activities in Palestine resulting in the lack of national leadership at the time of the partition. The newly formed League of Arab Nations was riddled with Arab rivalries interested in expanding the territory of their newly formed countries. The Arab League took control of the resistance to the establishment of a Jewish state and sidelined the Palestinians. The Arab invasion of Israel was never intended to liberate the Palestinians. It was motivated by the desire for territorial expansion. The failed attempt to "liberate Palestine" resulted in 520,000 to 1,000,000 Palestinian refugees dispersed between five different countries. Israel expelled 100,000 Palestinians into parts of Palestine held by Transjordan and Egypt and into Lebanon. Israel, as well as the Arab countries where Palestinians fled, worked to prevent the reemergence of Palestinian national identity (The Palestinians).

Occupied West Bank

In the war of 1948, Jordan gained control of the Old City of Jerusalem and the entire west bank of the Jordan River (West Bank). On April 24, 1950, Jordan annexed the West Bank, and the Palestinians were given Jordanian citizenship and allotted 30 seats in parliament. These 30 seats remained until 1988 when Jordan ceded its right to the West Bank. In

1967, Israel took control of East Jerusalem and the West Bank. As a result, 240,000 Palestinians again became refugees (most were absorbed by Jordan). Another 600,000 Palestinians were now under Israeli Military Occupation.

Military Occupation

When an armed force holds territory beyond its own borders, the term "occupation" applies. There are international laws that apply to "occupied" territories. In the case of the West Bank, Israel did not annex the territory but governed (occupied) through a military presence, and military orders became the law. Under the Interim Agreement between Israel and the Palestine Liberation Organization of September 28, 1995, those areas from which Israel has withdrawn its military forces are no longer considered "occupied" by Israel. However, according to the Agreement, there is a continued presence of Israeli troops.

What is a Palestinian?

"What's a Palestinian? There is no such thing as a Palestinian." This was Golda Meir's response to a reporter, after the war of 1967, when he asked, "What about the Palestinian?" Like most evangelical Christians, I accepted this response as truth until 1996 when the Lord called me to work among the Palestinians. I served with my Christian Palestinian brothers and sisters for three and a half years. During this time, the Lord shared with me His heart for the Palestinians, and many of the Palestinians, also, shared their hearts with me.

One example of their sharing comes from Katie, a student in the extension campus I pioneered in East Jerusalem. The class had been going through a video series from the main campus on the book of Ephesians. It was a wonderful study and everyone was being so blessed by the rich teaching of God's word. On the afternoon of the final session, at the very end of the video, the instructor went off on a tangent about the Palestinians—it was not nice. Silence hung in the room as the students tried to process what they had just heard from an instructor they had grown to love and respect over the course of the semester. I turned off the video and asked if they would like to talk about what they had just heard.

Katie, who is the wife of a pastor, started to speak, and as she spoke, she started to cry. "They don't care about us," she cried. [*They*—meaning the Christians from the Western world.] "They come here in full planes every day, and they don't care about us. They only care about the Jews, and the Jews do not even believe in Jesus. We are their brothers and sisters, and they don't care about us."

Katie's words have echoed in my mind for the many years since that afternoon. It is for Katie and all my wonderful Palestinian brothers and sisters that I am adding this chapter. Usually, when I teach this course, on the last class I will share about the Christian Palestinians and ask the students to commit to a time of prayer for them. I am asking you, as a reader, to do the same. Please pray for the Christian Palestinians.

Who Are the Palestinians?

Golda Meir's response to the reporter was not just a flippant remark but was an actual policy of Israel until 1993. It was illegal, in the occupied territories, to write the name Palestine, to have any textbooks or any other written material that had the name Palestine written on it. Yet, when Israel became established as a state, it did so in a geographical area, that since the time of the Roman Empire, was known as Palestine. The indigenous population of this geographical area was known as Palestinians. Imagine, if you possibly can, what it would be like for you if you were told (and had it enforced) that there was no such thing as an American, or a European. Furthermore, any attempt you made to connect with your heritage would result in your arrest. This was the reality for Palestinians living under Israeli military occupation.

One cannot consider modern Israel without considering the Palestinians. The name Palestine was given to Israel after the Romans expelled the Jews from their homeland. The population at that time was a mix of Jews, Christians, and pagans. They became known as Palestinians (135 AD). Under the Roman Empire, Palestine was incorporated into the province of Syria, as was previously mentioned. From 1948 until present day, this geographical area became known once again as Israel. Yet, within the borders of Modern Israel and the Occupied Territories, there were and is today an indigenous population known as the Palestinians.

Christian Palestinians

Palestinian Christians have existed in Israel since the Day of Pentecost. In 1947, a little less than 10% of Palestinians were Christians. Today their numbers have dropped to around 4%. Many of these are Evangelical Christians who are committed to reaching both Jews and Muslims with the Gospel. These Evangelical Christians are a minority within the state of Israel because they are Arabs. They are a minority among the Arabs because they are Christians, and they are a minority among the Christians because they are Protestant Evangelicals. Daily life for an Evangelical Christian in Israel is challenging to say the least.

Christian Palestinian Organizations in Israel

The Palestinian Bible Society (PBS) is an evangelical organization that is not only involved in the distribution of Bibles and Christian material, they also have many evangelical outreaches specific to age and need, including at the Israeli checkpoints. The PBS coordinates efforts with other Christian organizations and works together with the Bible Society in Israel.

The Jerusalem Evangelical Organization (JEO) is (as the name suggests) an evangelical organization that focuses primarily on the traditional Christian and the Muslim communities. Their work involves mercy ministries, Christian filmmaking, and the distribution of Christian material.

Ma'a Salam is based in Bethlehem. The focus of their ministry is reconciliation between Arab and Jews. They arrange events for Arab-Christians and Israeli Believers. Among the events they sponsor is a week of camping in the desert for youth from both groups mentioned.

These are only a few of the many Palestinian-Christian Organizations and churches working in Israel, the West Bank, and Gaza to bring the gospel to unsaved Jews, Muslims, and traditional Christians. They need our prayer and encouragement.

DISCUSSION POINTS:
- Does the content of prophecy automatically have God's approval?
- It was prophesied that Jesus would be put to death. If you were living at the time of Christ, would you have participated in His crucifixion because it was prophesied?
- Do the modern nation of Israel and their policies concerning the Palestinians reflect the character of God?
- Believers are encouraged to pray for the peace of Jerusalem, how do you envision that prayer being answered?

Arab-Israeli Conflict

The conflict between the Arabs and Israel changed significantly in 1967 when Israel gained the West Bank and Gaza. With the majority of the Palestinians coming under the authority of Israel, the conflict became an internal one. From 1967 until 1987, the Israeli authorities issued 1,200 military orders which controlled every aspect of the Palestinians daily life. On the Palestinian universities, a struggle for national identity began to gain momentum. The Student Senate and the Palestinian community expected the universities to propagate Palestinian culture. Israeli Military Orders forbid anything related to the name or concept of Palestine.

The Israelis viewed the universities on the West Bank as hotbeds for terrorism. The students viewed the universities as being the first Palestinian national institutions, and as such, they were expected to be very much a part of the national struggle. The Israeli authorities believed that the PLO was the guiding force behind the student demonstrations and issued military orders that outlawed any printed material with the word Palestine. The students had begun to gather around the flagpole on campus and sing the Palestinian national anthem. This was outlawed and the Israeli military would surround the campus to enforce the "law". In response, the students would throw stones at the soldiers. The military would then fire canisters of gas and live ammunition onto the campus. These conflicts developed into the first *Intifada*. The word *intifada* in Arabic means the "shaking off" and referred to the Israeli occupation.

The students' movement developed into an organized resistance movement on the West Bank and in Gaza. The Palestinians had no access to weapons so they used stones. The Intifada was fought by stone-throwing students and youth for five years. They were successful in bringing the Israelis to the table for peace talks.

The Madrid Conference of 1991 was a peace conference held in Madrid. It was an attempt by the international community to revive the Israeli-Palestinian peace process. The Madrid Peace Conference led the way to the Oslo Accords of 1993-1995. The Oslo Accords was a peace process aimed at achieving a peace-treaty which recognized the "right of the Palestinian people to self-determination". The Palestinian Authority was created with the limited authority over parts of the West Bank and Gaza Strip. Arafat and his army returned to the West Bank and a new era in Palestinian and Israeli relations was ushered in.

In 2000, the Second Intifada erupted in response to Ariel Sharon visiting the Temple Mount—this was seen by Palestinians as being highly provocative. This is also referred to as the al-Aqsa Intifada because this is the place where the Intifada started. This uprising lasted until 2005 and resulted in the construction of the Israeli West Bank barrier wall and Israel's withdrawal from the Gaza Strip. The Intifadas were followed by the Gaza-Israeli wars.

Palestinian militant actions escalated in the Gaza Strip following the election to government of the Islamic political party Hamas in 2005. Under the 2005 disengagement plan, Israel retained exclusive control over Gaza's airspace and territorial waters, continued to patrol and monitor the external land perimeter of the Gaza Strip, and continued to monitor and blockade Gaza's coastline. When the Islamic party Hamas gained the majority of seats in the government, the Gaza conflict between Israel and Gaza intensified. Palestinians began shooting rockets at Israeli settlements located near the Gaza border, and staged cross-border raids and large scale conventional warfare began beyond the peripheries of Gaza. In 2007, the entire Gaza Strip came under the control of the Hamas government after coup d'état rocket attacks from Gaza increased. In 2008, there was a cease-fire for the Gaza area. Israel broke the cease fire and attacked—the target of the raid was the tunnels the Hamas used to enter into Israel. Hamas fired 50-70 rockets into Israel.

Israel launched a ground invasion in 2009. In 2010, two Israeli soldiers were killed during a conflict with Gaza. This was the first time Israeli soldiers were killed by hostile fire in or around Gaza. In 2011, Israel initiated operation "Returning Echo" in response to the continued rocketing and incursions from Gaza. Each year since has been filled with rocket attacks, cross-border attacks and conventional wars; the most recent was in 2014 when Israel launched Operation Protective Edge in which more than 2,100 Palestinians were killed. The 50-day war came to an end on August 26, 2014 when a ceasefire was agreed upon.

Pray for the Peace of Jerusalem

Truly no man can bring about peace between the Arabs and the Jews. There is too much history, too many memories of atrocities committed, and too many religious fanatics. The three and a half years of peace mentioned in prophecy will be miraculous, and it is easy to see why it would unravel so quickly. The only hope for peace in Jerusalem is when Jesus Christ returns to establish His Kingdom reign—pray for the peace of Jerusalem!

REFERENCES

Karni, L. A. (1999). *Bethlehem University: A case study in the development of higher education in the midst of political struggle.* Jerusalem, IL: www.leonakarni.com. (listed under "Writings").

Khalidi, R. (1997). *Palestinian identity: The construction of modern national consciousness.* New York, NY: Columbia University Press.

Kimmerling, B. & Migdal, J. S. (1994). *Palestinians: The making of a people.* Cambridge, MA: Harvard University Press.

Morris, B. (1994). *The birth of the Palestinian refugee problem, 1947-1949.* Cambridge, MA: Cambridge University Press.

Muslih, M. Y. (1988). *The origins of Palestinian Nationalism.* New York, NY: Columbia University Press.

Shehadeh, R. (1980). *The West Bank and the rule of law: A study.* Ramallah, IL: The International Commission of Jurists.

Made in the USA
Middletown, DE
14 July 2023

35193441R00146